"George Lakoff serves progressives well by explaining how language and moral framing equals power in politics. *Thinking Points* helps leaders and activists alike to turn this knowledge into a compelling vision for society."

—John Podesta, CEO and President,
Center for American Progress

"*Thinking Points* is a must-read for anyone who doesn't want speaking out to become a dying art."   —Arianna Huffington

"Lakoff has done it again. In *Thinking Points*, the good professor and the Rockridge Institute team have connected a broad progressive policy vision to fundamental American values. It's time for progressives to get off defense and go on offense. By laying the foundations of progressive policy in the traditional American values of freedom, responsibility, and care for others, George Lakoff and Rockridge have shown us how. This is the must-read progressive-message handbook."   —Wes Boyd, MoveOn.org

"In *Thinking Points*, George Lakoff and the Rockridge Institute show how progressives can stop appealing to some hypothetical 'middle' and instead appeal to the deep morality that the vast majority of Americans share. When we speak from our hearts, the integrity of this will speak broadly."

—Joan Blades, MoveOn.org

"In an environment too often dominated by sound-bite arguments and political polarization, *Thinking Points* is more than a communications tool; it is a must-read for progressives as well as for nonpartisan activist organizations like the ACLU that want to trumpet their values not only loudly, but effectively. Professor Lakoff's expertise has been invaluable in articulating the ACLU's core values—fundamentally *American* values—to a broad and politically diverse audience."

—Anthony D. Romero, Executive Director, American Civil Liberties Union

"This book is essential reading for anyone who wants to speak out effectively about progressive American values."

—Eli Pariser, Executive Director, MoveOn.org Political Action

THINKING POINTS

ALSO BY GEORGE LAKOFF

Whose Freedom?:
The Battle over America's Most Important Idea

Don't Think of an Elephant!:
Know Your Values and Frame the Debate

Moral Politics: How Liberals and Conservatives Think

Metaphors We Live By

More Than Cool Reason: A Field Guide to Poetic Metaphor

Philosophy in the Flesh:
The Embodied Mind and Its Challenge to Western Thought

Where Mathematics Comes From:
How the Embodied Mind Brings Mathematics into Being

Women, Fire, and Dangerous Things:
What Categories Reveal About the Mind

THINKING POINTS

COMMUNICATING OUR AMERICAN

VALUES AND VISION

A PROGRESSIVE'S HANDBOOK

GEORGE LAKOFF

AND THE ROCKRIDGE INSTITUTE

FARRAR, STRAUS AND GIROUX / NEW YORK

Farrar, Straus and Giroux
19 Union Square West, New York 10003

Copyright © 2006 by Tides Center/Rockridge Institute
All rights reserved
Distributed in Canada by Douglas & McIntyre Ltd.
Printed in the United States of America
First edition, 2006

Library of Congress Control Number: 2006932396

ISBN-13: 978-0-374-53090-7
ISBN-10: 0-374-53090-4

Designed by Jonathan L. Lippincott

www.fsgbooks.com

1   3   5   7   9   10   8   6   4   2

CONTENTS

CONTRIBUTORS

Bruce Budner, Executive Director
Kevin Budner, Research Assistant
Kyra Davis, Research Assistant
Mark Ettlinger, Senior Researcher
Sam Ferguson, Senior Researcher
George Lakoff, Founder and Senior Fellow
Arianna Siegel, Research Assistant
Jessica Thierman, Research Assistant

PREFACE

America today is in danger. It faces the threat of domination by a radical, authoritarian right wing that refers to itself as "conservative," as if it were preserving and promoting American values. In fact, it has been trampling on them.

American values are inherently progressive, but progressives have lost their way. As traditional Americans, that is, as progressive Americans, we are beginning to lose our identity, the very values that have made America a great and free country—a country where tolerance has led us to unity, where diversity has given us strength, where acting for the common good has brought our dreams to fruition, and where respect for human dignity has increased opportunity, released creativity, and generated wealth.

But progressives have so taken these values for granted that we no longer have the ability to articulate a progressive vision. We have lost hold of the terms of political debate, and even ceded the language of progressive ideals—like "freedom" and "liberty"—to redefinition by an extremist right wing. The radical right understands *its* values and knows *its* agenda. It has imposed *its* ideas and *its* language on America. It has dominated public debate, which has allowed it to seize power.

Progressive political leaders have been inhibited in creating long-term change by the short-term necessities of running for office and by the need to block disastrous legislation day after day without unified grassroots support. Progressive policy makers can do only so much in the present environment. It is up to the grass roots, outside the Beltway, to find its collective progressive voice, to call once more for the common good, and to form a chorus singing out America.

The Rockridge Institute is part of that chorus and is strongly committed to progressive American values and vision. This handbook is a reflection of our work and our commitment. Progressives feel in their gut what is right. Our job at Rockridge is to turn those feelings into language, to help find the frames that will make our truths visible to others, and to translate our overwhelming sense of what is right into effective arguments.

We perceived a need among grassroots progressives for a short, easy-to-read, systematic account of the progressive vision, for the principles that apply across issue areas, and for all the essentials of framing—a handbook that can be carried around in pocket or purse and accessed over the Internet. Here it is.

There is a lot we have tackled here. We wanted to learn why slogans and spin mostly don't work for progressives. We wanted to clarify the strict father/nurturant parent models, which have been widely misunderstood. We wanted to explain why voters don't respond to laundry lists of programs and policies. And we wanted to show why framing is necessary to serve the truth.

Along the way, we have introduced some new concepts. For instance, we present up-to-date research on *deep framing*—the moral values and political principles that cut across issues and that are required before any slogans or clever phrases can resonate with the public. We look at *argument frames*—the general overall structure of argument forms used by both liberals and conservatives. And we inquire as to why conservatives focus on direct causation while liberals see systemic, or complex, causation.

Most important, we examine and reject the idea of an ideological "center." It is not made up of "moderates," nor is it defined by issues spread across a left-to-right spectrum. Instead, the "center" is made up of *biconceptuals*. The idea of biconceptualism is essential to understanding—and changing—American politics. We explain why progressives can and should talk to biconceptuals in the same way they talk to their base.

A cautionary note about this handbook: Advocacy groups running specific ad campaigns, candidates running for office, and policy makers all have short-term needs—they want language for the next ad, for tomorrow's speech, and for the upcoming election campaign, and they want sound-bite responses to this morning's charges by the other side. This handbook is not about quick-and-dirty, short-term fixes to immediate tactical problems. It is about long-term strategy, a strategy for returning America to its progressive ideals. It is about changing the way we do politics. It is about helping America get in touch with its progressive roots.

We hope this handbook begins a process of creating a language of a renewed liberalism. In its online version, it will form the basis of the Rockridge Progressive Manual Project, designed to extend this handbook, step-by-step, to all issue areas, and to do so interactively, with an ongoing dialogue, a national conversation, with grassroots progressives. This handbook is also the seed of the Rockridge Action Network, a network of activists—individuals and groups—who want to speak out on issues and place progressive ideas and values before the public. Contact us online at info@rockridgeinstitute.org.

All over America, progressives are finding their voices. We hope this handbook will help you find yours.

George Lakoff
Berkeley, California
August 1, 2006

THINKING POINTS

INTRODUCTION: WHY WE WRITE

Progressives have a long and storied history in the United States. It is a narrative driven by the liberal principles of freedom, equality, human dignity, tolerance, and the celebration of diversity, and by the conviction that our common wealth should be used for the common good. Our nation's greatest moments occurred when these principles prevailed. We write so that they may endure.

These principles belong to no person, place, or party. They belong to no race, class, or gender. They belong to no time, region, or country of origin. And they recognize no red state/blue state dichotomy. We write to remind ourselves of the progressive principles that have always lifted our nation to higher moral ground. And we reflect on our past in the hope that we can leave our children with a better future.

Our greatest patriots have been those who articulated and acted on these principles. They gave life to our Constitution through their courage and their convictions. Their legacy is our proudest common heritage. It humbles us. We write so we, too, may act on our deepest convictions.

The central protagonists in this story have been citizens. First and foremost, the revolutionaries, like George Washington and Thomas Jefferson, who fought for the expansion of freedoms by inciting a revolt and throwing off the yoke of British despotism. In their footsteps came the abolitionists, like Frederick Douglass and Harriet Tubman, who insisted that no democracy could respectfully call itself one so long as slavery—the nation's "original sin"—endured. Following them were the suffragists, like Susan B. Anthony and Elizabeth Cady Stanton, who expanded our understanding of equality and won for women the right to vote.

There are others. The Reverend Martin Luther King Jr. and Rosa Parks marched for tolerance and inspired the nation to celebrate diversity. Mother Jones, Cesar Chavez, and Sojourner Truth—while living in different times—championed the inalienable dignity of all human beings. John Muir and Rachel Carson gave voice to the natural world and to our commons. In the name of peace and a check on overreaching executive power, Daniel Ellsberg released the Pentagon Papers and hastened an end to the Vietnam War.

Great politicians deserve our praise for showing their vision and their courage in the face of adversity. Abraham Lincoln freed the slaves and saved our union. Theodore Roosevelt established a role for government to curb the unbridled excesses of the market and protect our natural wonders. Franklin Delano Roosevelt went a step further and permanently established government's central role in using the common wealth for the common good by launching the New Deal. It was more than a set of programs—it was a movement imbued with the core progressive values of empathy and responsibility, with the idea that government should not only care about people but also act on that caring.

The beliefs, the convictions, the *values* that inspired these patriots can inspire us today. While the issues and challenges we face are different, the guiding principles remain.

If America were as these patriots envisioned it, there would be no reason for *Thinking Points*. Unfortunately, the nation has strayed far from its progressive values. Children remain impoverished, without adequate food and health care, offending our commitment to basic human dignity. State-sanctioned discrimination against homosexuality pervades, mocking our commitment to diversity, tolerance, and equality before the law. Wide disparities persist between ethnic communities—in health, education, incarceration rates, and economic power—leaving the promise of the civil rights movement unfulfilled. A global climate crisis looms, the challenge to solve it still unmet. And we are stuck in a military quagmire in Iraq that has sapped our nation not only of its strength and its wealth but of its very moral fiber.

Above all, a dark cloud of authoritarianism looms over the nation, making it difficult to address any of these issues without major political change. Radical conservatives have taken over the reins of government and have been controlling the terms of political debate for many years. For real change to happen, progressive ideals must return to center stage in our national political discourse. This will be neither easy nor quick—it will take years of work. But we can prevail.

It is up to us—citizens—to articulate the progressive vision. Progressive political leaders cannot do it alone. For all of their intelligence and good intentions, they are subject to overwhelming short-term pressures. They will need the help of progressives throughout America. We must trumpet our values throughout the nation so that progressive political leaders will have the backing they need to speak out far more freely.

Fortunately, today, in the service of these ideals, we do not face a British army, as the revolutionaries did. We do not face lynch mobs, as the abolitionists and civil rights workers did. We do not face a Pinkerton army, as striking workers once did. We face ourselves. We must muster the political courage to voice—and to stand for—what we most deeply believe. This is why we write. We hope you will use *Thinking Points* to help return our country to its progressive ideals.

1

WINNING AND LOSING

Richard Wirthlin, chief strategist for former president Ronald Reagan, made a discovery in 1980 that profoundly changed American politics. As a pollster, he was taught that people vote for candidates on the basis of the candidates' positions on issues. But his initial polls for Reagan revealed something fascinating: Voters who didn't agree with Reagan on the issues still wanted to vote for him. Mystified, Wirthlin studied the matter further. He discovered just what made people want to vote for Reagan.[1]

Reagan talked about *values* rather than issues. Communicating values mattered more than specific policy positions. Reagan *connected* with people; he communicated well. Reagan also appeared *authentic*—he seemed to believe what he said. And because he talked about his values, connected with people, and appeared authentic, they felt they could *trust* him.

For these four reasons—values, connection, authenticity, and trust—voters *identified* with Reagan; they felt he was one of them. It was not because all of his values matched theirs exactly. It was not because he was from their socioeconomic class or subculture. It was because they believed in the integrity of his connection with them as well as the connection between his worldview and his actions.

Issues are real, as are the facts of the matter. But issues are also symbolic of values and of trustworthiness. Effective campaigns must communicate the candidates' values and use issues symbolically—as indicative of their moral values and their trustworthiness.

Recall Reagan's mythical Cadillac-driving "welfare queen." For Reagan, she represented more than just a case of welfare abuse. She came to symbolize all that was wrong with the government's approach to dealing with poverty, especially a wide array of government "handouts"—programs he thought rewarded laziness, removed the incentive to be disciplined, and promoted immorality.

Whatever we may think of Reagan, this has been a winning formula for conservatives for the past quarter century. Progressives need to learn from it. Politics is about values; it is about communication; it is about voters trusting a candidate to do what is right; it is about believing in, and identifying with, a candidate's worldview. And it is about symbolism.

Issues are secondary—not irrelevant or unimportant, but secondary. A position on issues should follow from one's values, and the choice of issues and policies should symbolize those values.

One misunderstanding, common among progressive circles, is that the Reagan and George W. Bush elections were about "personality" rather than anything substantive. Nothing is more substantive than a candidate's moral worldview—and whether he or she authentically abides by it.

Wirthlin's discovery happened to be about a presidential candidate, but it applies much more broadly. It should be taken to heart by all progressives: Concentrate on values and principles. Be authentic; stand up for what you really believe. Empathize and connect with the people you are talking to, on the basis of identity—their identity and yours.

This book is not about winning and losing elections. It is about winning and losing hearts and minds. This can happen only by helping people discover who they truly are in their heart of hearts.

It is about values and how to communicate them. It is about what a progressive vision is, about what fundamental progressive moral values and principles are, and about how one can articulate them and argue persuasively in favor of them. The secret is effective communication—the use of words and language in the service of our deepest convictions.

Progressives have not only failed to understand Wirthlin's discovery, they have also not understood recent advances in cognitive science, so they continue to fall into a number of traps. These are traps of our own making, however, and we can get out of them without having to change anything about our values.

This is cause for optimism. The purpose of this handbook is to lay out the anatomy of progressive values, ideas, and arguments to free us from traps we have fallen into.

TWELVE TRAPS TO AVOID

1. The Issue Trap. We hear it said all the time: Progressives won't unite behind any set of ideas. We all have different ideas and care about different issues. The truth is that progressives *do* agree at the level of *values* and that there is a real basis for progressive unity. Progressive values cut across issues. So do principles and forms of argument. Conservatives argue conservatism, no matter what the issue. Progressives should argue progressivism. We need to get out of *issue silos* that isolate arguments and keep us from the values and principles that define an overall progressive vision.

2. The Poll Trap. Many progressives slavishly follow polls. The job of leaders is to lead, not follow. Besides, contrary to popular belief, polls in themselves do not present accurate empirical evidence. Polls are only as accurate as the framing of their questions, which is often inadequate. Real leaders don't use polls to find out what positions to take; they lead people to new positions.

3. The Laundry List Trap. Progressives tend to believe that people vote on the basis of lists of programs and policies. In fact, people vote based on values, connection, authenticity, trust, and identity.

4. The Rationalism Trap. There is a commonplace—and false—theory that reason is completely conscious, literal (applies directly to the objective world), logical, universal, and unemotional. Cognitive science has shown that every one of these assumptions is false. These assumptions lead progressives into other traps: assuming that hard facts will persuade voters, that voters are "rational" and vote in their self-interest and on the issues, and that negating a frame is an effective way to argue against it.

5. The No-Framing-Necessary Trap. Progressives often argue that "truth doesn't need to be framed" and that the "facts speak for themselves." People use frames—deep-seated mental structures about how the world works—to understand facts. Frames are in our brains and define our common sense. It is impossible to think or communicate without activating frames, and so which frame is activated is of crucial importance. Truths need to be framed appropriately to be seen as truths. Facts need a context.

6. The Policies-Are-Values Trap. Progressives regularly mistake policies with values, which are ethical ideas like empathy, responsibility, fairness, freedom, justice, and so on. Policies are not themselves values, though they are, or should be, *based* on values. Thus, Social Security and universal health insurance are not values; they are policies meant to reflect and codify the values of human dignity, the common good, fairness, and equality.

7. The Centrist Trap. There is a common belief that there is an ideological "center"—a large group of voters either with a consistent ideology of their own or lined up left to right on the issues or forming a "mainstream," all with the same positions on issues. In fact, the so-called center is actually made up of *biconceptuals*, people who are conservative in some aspects of life and progressive in others. Voters who self-identify as "conservative" often have significant progressive values in important areas of life. We should address these "partial progressive" biconceptuals through their progressive identities, which are often systematic and extensive.

A common mistaken ideology has convinced many progressives that they must "move to the right" to get more votes. In reality, this is counterproductive. By moving to the right, progressives actually help activate the right's values and give up on their own. In the process, they also alienate their base.

8. The "Misunderestimating" Trap. Too many progressives think that people who vote conservative are just stupid, especially those who vote against their economic self-interest. Progressives believe that we only have to tell them the real economic facts, and they will change the way they vote. The reality is that those who vote conservative have their reasons, and we had better understand them. Conservative populism is *cultural*—not economic—in nature. Conservative populists see themselves as oppressed by elitist liberals who look down their noses at them, when they are just ordinary, moral, right-thinking folks. They see liberals as trying to impose an immoral "political correctness" on them, and they are angry about it.

Progressives also paint conservative leaders as incompetent and not very smart, based on a misunderstanding of the conservative agenda. This results from looking at conservative goals through progressive values. Looking at conservative goals through conservative values yields insight and shows just how effective conservatives really are.[2]

9. The Reactive Trap. For the most part, we have been letting conservatives frame the debate. Conservatives are taking the initiative on policy making and getting their ideas out to the public. When progressives *react*, we echo the conservative frames and values, so our message is not heard or, even worse, reinforces their ideas. Progressives need a collection of *proactive* policies and communication techniques to get our own values out on our own terms. "War rooms" and "truth squads" must *change* frames, not reinforce conservative frames. But even then, they are not nearly enough. Progressive leaders, *outside of any party*, must come together in an ongoing, long-term, organized national campaign that honestly conveys progressive values to the public—day after day, week after week, year after year, no matter what the specific issues of the day are.

10. The Spin Trap. Some progressives believe that winning elections or getting public support is a matter of clever spin and catchy slogans—what we call "surface framing." Surface framing is meaningless without deep framing—our deepest moral convictions and political principles. Framing, used honestly at both the deep and surface levels, is needed to make the truth visible and our values clear.

Spin, on the other hand, is the dishonest use of surface linguistic frames to hide the truth. And progressive values and principles—the deep frames—must be in place before slogans can have an effect; slogans alone accomplish nothing. Conservative slogans work because they have been communicating their deep frames for decades.

11. The Policyspeak Trap. Progressives consistently use legislative jargon and bureaucratic solutions, like "Medicare prescription drug benefits," to speak to the public about their positions. Instead, progressives should speak in terms of the common concerns of voters—for instance, how a policy will let you send your daughter to college, or how it will let you launch your own business.

12. The Blame Game Trap. It is convenient to blame our

problems on the media and on conservative lies. Yes, conservative leaders have regularly lied and used Orwellian language to
distort the truth, and yes, the media have been lax, repeating the
conservatives' frames. But we have little control over that. We
can control only how *we* communicate. Simply correcting a lie
with the truth is not enough. We must reframe from our moral
perspective so that the truth can be understood. This reframing
is needed to get our deep frames into public discourse. If enough
people around the country honestly, effectively, and regularly express a progressive vision, the media will be much more likely to
adopt *our* frames.

Looking at these traps, we might think we have dug ourselves
in too deep. At Rockridge, we don't think so. Why are we
optimistic? Because there is a clear path out of all these traps:
understanding the anatomy of the progressive vision and understanding the anatomy of the electorate.

Once we grasp that, helping American voters find their progressive hearts will be a little easier.

2

BICONCEPTUALISM

Understanding whom we are talking to—and whom we *want* to talk to—is crucial before progressives begin to articulate what it is they have to say and how best to say it. This is true for progressive candidates as well as activists and activist groups. The real challenge in this area is twofold: First, we want to activate our base while reaching swing voters at the same time; second, we want to do so without having to lie, distort, mislead, or pretend to be something we aren't.

The pressure to dissemble comes from certain commonplace myths about swing voters and the "center." So for starters, let's put to rest the notion of the political or ideological "center"—it doesn't exist. Instead, what we have are biconceptuals—of many kinds.

When it comes to progressive and conservative worldviews, we are all biconceptuals. You may live by progressive values in most areas of your life, but if you see Rambo movies and *understand* them, you have a *passive* conservative worldview allowing you to make sense of them. Or you may be a conservative, but if you appreciated *The Cosby Show*, you were using a *passive* progressive worldview. Movies and television aside, what we are really interested in are *active* biconceptuals—people who use one moral system in one area and the other moral system in another area of their political thinking.

Biconceptualism makes sense from the perspective of the brain and the mechanism of neural computation. The progressive and conservative worldviews are mutually exclusive. But in a human brain, both can exist side by side, each neurally inhibiting the other and structuring different areas of experience.[1] It is hardly unnatural—or unusual—to be fiscally conservative and socially progressive, or to support a liberal domestic policy and a conservative foreign policy, or to have a conservative view of the market and a progressive view of civil liberties.

Political biconceptuals are commonplace, and they include those who identify themselves as having a single ideology. Biconceptuals are not to be confused with "moderates." There is no moderate worldview, and very few people are genuine moderates. True moderates look for linear scales and take positions in the middle of those scales. How much should we pay to improve schools? A lot? A little? "A moderate amount" is what a true "moderate" would say. Such folks may exist, but moderation is not a political ideology. Nor is the use of two strongly opposed ideologies in different arenas a matter of "moderation." It is biconceptualism.

PARTIAL CONSERVATIVES

Consider Senator Joe Lieberman of Connecticut, who describes himself as a moderate. In fact, little about him is moderate. He doesn't typically stake out middle-of-the-road positions on particular issues. Instead, his politics include both liberal and conservative positions, but on different issues. This makes him a biconceptual. His progressive worldview appears in his staunch support of environmental protection, abortion rights, and workers' rights.[2] His conservative worldview emerges in areas like his support of faith-based initiatives, school vouchers, and most notably, the current policy on Iraq.[3] Because he tends to adopt progressive positions more often than conservative ones, we refer to him as a "partial conservative."

Many liberals are biconceptual. The "cold war liberals" were divided between a progressive domestic policy and a conservative foreign policy based on using force—or the threat of it—to further the nation's military, economic, and political strength. Other Democrats may be economic progressives and social conservatives, or vice versa. Unions, for instance, have genuinely progressive goals but are often organized and run in a strict way. "Militant" progressives commonly have strict means and nurturant ends, while courtly, gentlemanly and ladylike conservatives may have nurturant means and strict ends. Such a split between means and ends is not unusual.

PARTIAL PROGRESSIVES

Similarly, within the wide range of those who tend toward a conservative worldview, many are "partial progressives." If we want to communicate with these conservatives, we'd better recognize that they may live by the progressive moral system in extremely important areas of their lives.

In fact, their progressive values may be their defining characteristics, who they most essentially are—even if they do not see themselves as progressives or liberals. Let's look at five of the more common types of "partially progressive conservatives" and see how their values match up with those of self-defined progressives.

Lovers of the land. A lot of conservatives may be hunters and fishermen (who want to fish in unpolluted waters so they can eat their catch); they may be cyclists, hikers, and campers who love to take their families to the national parks; they may be farmers or ranchers who are viscerally connected to their land; or they may be devout Christians who take seriously their biblical obligation to be stewards of the earth. They might never call themselves "environmentalists" or toss around words like "sustainability" or "biodiversity," but they share many of the same values—values that are ultimately progressive.

Communitarians. There are conservatives who believe in progressive communities. Across the nation, for instance, self-styled conservatives often live in communities—rural towns or suburban neighborhoods—where leaders care about people and act responsibly, where everyone looks out for one another, cares about one another, helps others in need, provides community service, and emphasizes progressive empathy and social responsibility instead of conservative strictness and individualism. They may thus be conservative in their national voting patterns and yet progressive in their communities.

People of faith. A sizable chunk of Americans who are conservative in certain parts of their lives are also progressive in their religion. For instance, religious Christians, both Catholics and Protestants, are progressives at heart if they believe they should live their lives according to the teachings of Christ—help the poor, feed the hungry, cure the sick, forgive the sinner, turn the other cheek. They will most likely see God as nurturant and loving, not strict and punitive. Even evangelicals (like former president Jimmy Carter) are often progressive.

Socially conscious employers. Many conservative entrepreneurs run their companies as progressive businesses—whether they see it that way or not. They treat their employees well, pay living wages and offer decent benefits, would not dream of harming the environment or their customers, and believe other businesses should also practice a morality that extends beyond just maximizing profit and following the letter of the law.

Civil libertarians. Some of the most ardent civil libertarians in America identify themselves as conservatives or simply as libertarians. They believe in the Bill of Rights and especially the

Fourth Amendment. They want their privacy protected and don't want the government spying on them or interfering with personal moral decisions or with their sex lives. They want free speech and freedom of association and want the government to stay out of religion and religion to stay out of government. They want constraints on the powers of the police and want strong protections from the courts. On issues of personal freedom, they abide by progressive morality.

Understanding this opens up a powerful way for progressives to communicate with swing voters on the basis of real shared values.

THE MYTHICAL CENTER

This critical understanding of biconceptuals has been obscured for many years by an obsession with the proverbial ideological "center," occupied by the people whose votes are needed by progressives and conservatives in order to win. Myths of the center come in a number of forms, which lead to counterproductive political strategies.

The four predominant myths of the center—the Label myth, the Linear myth, the Moderate myth, and the Mainstream myth—all assume that people vote on the basis of a candidate's positions on the issues. On the other hand, the biconceptual theory assumes that people vote according to the Wirthlin theory (see Chapter 1): on the basis of values, connection, authenticity, trust, and identity with issues used symbolically to reflect values.

The *Label myth* is the most vacuous. It asks voters to ascribe one of three labels to themselves: liberal, moderate, conservative. There is no content to these labels; they are empirically empty. There is no singular or definable "moderate" ideology or worldview, no consistency to what "moderates" believe. It is just a label of self-identification. Centrist Democrats William Galston and Elaine Kamarck adopt this theory in a widely publicized report, "The Politics of Polarization."[4] They use the self-identification percentages from 2004—liberal, 21 percent; moderate, 45 percent; conservative, 34 percent—and assume that those who self-identified as "liberal" have a progressive ideology and those who saw themselves as "conservative" have a conservative ideology. This, they argue, means that if thoroughgoing liberals remain true to their values, they will fail to persuade any but the staunch liberals. Instead, progressives must move to the "center" on issues to attract more "moderates," since they need a large majority of them to win.

On the surface, this may seem reasonable. But there is a significant problem with their methodology, a problem that psychologists have been dealing with for decades: There is a difference between self-identified labels and personal cognition. For example, there was no real change in sexual orientation that correlated with a rise in the number of people who self-identify as "gay" or "lesbian." Instead, there was a *change in attitude* about that label.

Similarly, in recent years, conservatives have negatively branded the word "liberal," and that is what is reflected in the 2004 poll, not the actual beliefs of Americans. The opposite is probably the case with the "moderate" label. "Moderates" are viewed as reasonable, unbiased, temperate, and balanced—all positive connotations, which may explain why people choose that label over the others. One remedy to this pitfall is careful investigation of voters' worldview and values and not just their self-identifying labels. Such an empirical approach to voter cognition is rarely taken in progressive polling, though there are certain exceptions.

The "center," according to the *Linear myth*, is based on a curious metaphor. It conceives of citizens as lined up left to right, with some on the extreme ends and others in between, with their locations determined by their positions on individual issues. This myth lurks behind the idea of the "center" and fosters the belief that progressives must move toward the right and abandon—or hide—their progressive ideology if they are to succeed. The theory is that moving rightward leaves more voters to the left of the candidate, making the candidate appear more, well, "moderate." This runs contrary to the biconceptual view that it is best to communicate and appeal to swing voters by activating their partial progressive identities with a progressive vision and appropriate progressive language.

The strategic—and ethical—problems that the Linear myth causes are extremely significant. "Moving to the right" means becoming inauthentic, and voters can smell a lack of authenticity. It means offending your base. It means lending credence to conservative issues and values. Remember, conservatives did not become successful by "moving to the left." They became successful by activating the conservative worldview—speaking the language of the base and inhibiting the liberal worldview by sneeringly attacking liberals.

The *Moderate myth* sounds good until you think about it. It says that people who act with moderation in their lives—people who are reasonable, unbiased, temperate, coolheaded, and balanced, people who don't want to go too far one way or the other—have a political worldview structured by moderation, a choice of a midpoint on various scales. But as soon as you take this seriously, it becomes clear that there is no such political worldview—no coherent and consistent account of politics in which all possible issues are points on linear scales and moderates are in the middle on all scales. First, many cases are yes-or-no matters. No scales. Take some examples: Should there be a death penalty? You can't kill someone only a little, or in moderation. Should abortion be legal? What does it mean to speak of someone having an abortion in moderation? Assisted suicide?

What does moderation mean? Three strikes? Is it moderation to go for five strikes? Drill in the Arctic National Wildlife Refuge? Even "moderate" drilling is drilling. There is no in-between. People who self-identify as "moderates" appear not to be in-betweeners, but rather biconceptuals—conservative in some issue areas and progressive in others.

Last, the *Mainstream myth* assumes that there is a real center of public opinion as determined by polls on particular issues. David Sirota, a progressive commentator, illustrates this myth:

> On the Iraq war, for instance, polls show a majority of Americans want a timetable for drawing down troops. On economic policy, most Americans support stronger government regulations to protect citizens. On trade, polls show the public is widely suspicious of free-trade deals that have destabilized the middle class. And on health care, surveys show that about two-thirds of those asked want a government-guaranteed universal health-insurance system—even if it means tax increases.[5]

Sirota, turning a centrist mode of thought back on the centrists, argues that the real mainstream center is made up of people with these beliefs and that progressives can win if they follow these polls and take the same positions as the mainstream voters. However, as with the challenge of finding a family who has 2.3 children, if you look across enough issues, you may not actually find a person who holds every single view that the majority of Americans hold. This is because there is no ideology—no worldview—connecting the different positions reflected in the polls; it's just a list of issue positions, a product of number crunching. As previously illustrated, a great many voters do not resemble this mythical mainstream but are, instead, biconceptuals.

SPEAKING TO SWING VOTERS

Political reality is far more complicated than any of these myths allow. The biconceptual "center" actually includes partial conservatives, partial progressives, and undecideds (biconceptuals in nonpolitical areas of life but with no fixed moral views governing their politics). Conservatives have understood the "center" in this way, and they understand that biconceptuals have both worldviews. By using conservative language, and repeating it over and over, they activate the deeper conservative value system, not only in their base but in partial conservatives as well. They also use antiliberal language, repeating it over and over to inhibit progressive values. Conservatives who use this strategy do not have to give up their values or their authenticity. All they have to do is talk to the center the same way they talk to their base.

Progressives can do the same. They can talk to the center the same way they talk to their base, and activate progressive values and frames in biconceptual swing voters. This keeps the progressive base and activates the progressive values of not just conservatives who are partial progressives but also biconceptuals who are undecided. In short, they can effectively go after the voters in the middle without giving up their progressive values.

One other thing worth mentioning is that political operatives have also relied on the idea of single-issue voters—people who vote exclusively on a politician's stance on one issue. This does not counter the idea that people vote based on values and not issues. Instead, what we find is that the single issue in question is almost always symbolic of broader cultural and political values. Examples include progressive Catholics voting for anti-abortion conservatives and progressive Jews seeing the Iraq war as being pro-Israel and voting for conservative Republicans on the war issue. On the other hand, "moral issue" voters tend to support abortion or gay marriage because they support a strict father worldview.

Trying to court these single-issue voters by taking a position you don't believe will most likely backfire, because that issue will activate a larger system of values you do not have. And this leads us to the overarching topic of authenticity.

AUTHENTICITY

The moral of these myths is simple: Be authentic and stick to what you really believe. Changing to a position you do not believe not only lacks integrity, it's a flawed and ineffective political strategy. There are, of course, progressives who are truly biconceptual and are partial conservatives. Here, too, honesty—and authenticity—is the best policy. If you believe that the conservative perspective is more appropriate to some issue area, argue your case, but do so using the linguistic frames that best represent your larger values and worldview.

The prevalence of biconceptuality among voters requires us to consider the role of pragmatism in issue politics. There are two kinds of political pragmatists. Both are willing to compromise, but for different reasons.

The *authentic pragmatist* realizes you can't get everything you think is right, but you can get much or most of it through negotiation. The authentic pragmatist sticks to his or her values and works to satisfy them maximally. The *inauthentic pragmatist*, on the other hand, is willing to depart from his or her true values for the sake of political gain.

There is all the difference in the world between the two as political leaders, though they may vote the same way. The authentic pragmatist is maintaining a consistent moral vision, while the inauthentic pragmatist is surrendering his or her moral vision.

As Wirthlin discovered, authenticity matters in politics. When you surrender authenticity, you surrender your values, and you surrender trust.

When your values are not currently popular, being authentic means having courage. Being courageous does not mean being unwise, or offending one's constituents. This handbook is intended to help make the courageous successful by helping them understand *framing*.

3

FRAMES AND BRAINS

"Framing" is not primarily about politics or political messaging, or communication. It is far more fundamental than that: Frames are the mental structures that allow human beings to understand reality—and sometimes to create what we take to be reality.

But the discovery and use of frames does have an enormous bearing on politics. Given our media-obsessed, fast-paced, talking-points political culture, it's critical that we understand the nature of framing and how it can be used.

Political framing is really applied cognitive science. Frames facilitate our most basic interactions with the world—they structure our ideas and concepts, they shape the way we reason, and they even impact how we perceive and how we act. For the most part, our use of frames is unconscious and automatic—we use them without realizing it.

Erving Goffman, the distinguished sociologist, was one of the first to notice frames and the way they structure our interactions with the world. Goffman studied institutions, like hospitals and casinos, and conventionalized social behavior, like dating and shopping. He found something quite remarkable: Social institutions and situations are shaped by mental structures (frames), which then determine how we behave in those institutions and situations.[1]

To describe this phenomenon, he used the metaphor of "life as a play." For instance, consider the hospital frame, with its clearly defined roles: *doctor, surgeon, nurse, orderly, patient, visitor, receptionist, janitor*, and so on. There are locations where scenes play out: *the operating room, the emergency room, the recovery room, the waiting area*, and *patient rooms*. There are props: *the operating table, scalpels, bandages, wheelchairs*, and so on. And there are conventional actions: *operations, taking temperature and blood pressure, checking charts, emptying bedpans*, and so on.

The hospital frame also has an internal logic, because there are fixed relations and hierarchies among the roles: Doctors are superior to nurses, who are superior to orderlies; all surgeons are doctors, but not vice versa; surgeons perform operations in the operating room.

Conversely, the hospital frame rules out certain behavior, because it determines what is appropriate and what isn't: Orderlies or visitors do not perform operations; surgeons don't empty bedpans; operations are not performed in the waiting area; visitors bring flowers to the patients, but surgeons don't bring flowers to orderlies.

The scenarios also have a logic and a linear order: First you check in at the registration desk, then you're prepped for an operation before you are operated on; visitors are allowed after the operation. Checking in after your operation is ruled out by the logic of the frame.

All of us know thousands of such frames for everyday conventionalized activities, from dating to taking buses to getting money at an ATM to eating at a restaurant. Many frames come with language that is meaningless outside that frame: *surgeon, emergency room, waiter, bus driver, PIN*. Without operations, a surgeon would be meaningless. Just as a waiter would be without restaurants.

Similarly, frames structure our political institutions—elections, courts, and legislative and administrative structures. In the frame defining the Supreme Court, the semantic roles include a chief justice and eight associate justices. The scenario structure includes hearing cases, voting on them, and writing opinions, in that order. The props include robes, the courthouse, a gavel, and so on.

Political disputes are sometimes about how frames interact and whether one frame takes priority over another. Can the FBI search a congressman's office for evidence of corruption? That is, does the administration frame include law enforcement jurisdiction over Congress?

Frame structures also appear on a smaller scale. Charles Fillmore, one of the world's great linguists, has studied how everyday frames work at the level of sentences. The verb "accuse," for example, is defined with respect to an accusation frame, with semantic roles: accuser, accused, offense, and accusation. The accuser and accused are people (or metaphorical people, like corporations), the offense is an action, and the accusation is a speech act, in particular, a declaration. The offense is assumed by the accuser to be *bad*, that is, illegal or immoral, and the accuser is declaring that the accused did perform the offense.

For example, take this sentence: "The Democrats accused Bush of illegal spying on U.S. citizens." The accusers are the Democrats, the accused is the president, the offense is illegal spying on U.S. citizens, and the accusation is the act of declaring. The verb "accuse" is decomposed into two statements, one declared and one presupposed. The badness (illegality or immorality) of the offense is presupposed by the accuser, who is declaring that the accused did perform the offense.

The word "spying" also comes with a frame, in which there is a spy, a spied-upon person, and an act of spying, which is a surreptitious attempt by the spy to get incriminating or strategically useful information about the spied-upon person. The spy is not just monitoring another's activities; the spy's job is to actively look for anything that could be interpreted as suspicious or incriminating. In short, the spy is bringing his or her own framing to the everyday activities of the spied-upon person. An activity that is "innocent" from the perspective of the person performing it may be suspicious or incriminating to the spy.

What is interesting about the above sentence is that Bush did not deny that the spying took place. His defense is that it was neither illegal nor immoral, not in any way *bad*, but rather that it was *good*, part of carrying out his duty as commander in chief. In doing so, Bush is trying to undermine the frame—to make the frame not fit—rather than to accept the presupposition.

Goffman's institutional frames and Fillmore's sentence frames have the same structure: semantic roles, relations between those roles, a typical scenario.

The vast majority of work on framing within cognitive science and linguistics is devoted to everyday aspects of our lives.[2] Our central focus at the Rockridge Institute is to ask questions about framing and its relevance to politics: How can we apply the discoveries in linguistics and cognitive science to politics? Is framing ever used to serve political ends without public awareness? By reframing, can we help reveal important truths about political issues?[3]

DEEP FRAMES: "THE WAR ON TERROR"

Over the past thirty-five years, conservatives have spent more than $4 billion constructing a system of dozens of think tanks and training institutes, staffed by right-wing intellectuals. They have managed to dominate the framing of issues and have profoundly changed American politics in the process.

One way they have done this is through the effective use of *surface frames*, such as the mental structures associated with the "war on terror" frame. These frames build on *lexical frames*—the conceptual frames associated with words like "war" in its ordinary sense and "terror" in its ordinary sense. Surface frames are associated with phrases like "war on terror" that both activate and depend critically on *deep frames*. These are the most basic frames that constitute a moral worldview or a political philosophy. Deep frames define one's overall "common sense." Without deep frames, there is nothing for surface frames to hang on to. Slogans do not make sense without the appropriate deep frames in place.

A closer look at the "war on terror" frame can be illustrative. The American public has hardly grasped the significance of this conservative frame. In the immediate aftermath of 9/11, there was brief discussion of treating the terrorist acts as an international police problem (Secretary of State Colin Powell, for one, suggested this[4]): Take it to the International Criminal Court, seek an indictment of Osama bin Laden and other al-Qaeda operatives, forge an international coalition to find him and al-Qaeda members, devote our resources to diplomacy and intelligence gathering, and use our military for "police actions" if need be. In short, put bin Laden on trial for crimes against humanity and give him due punishment.

That idea didn't last long. Quite immediately, the Bush administration and the right-wing message machine started promoting a "war on terror." The conceptual frame associated with "war" has semantic roles: armies, a fight, a moral crusade, a commander in chief, a capture of territory, the surrender of an enemy, and patriots supporting the troops. "War" implies the necessity of military action. When we're in a war, all other concerns are secondary.

When "terror" is added to "war," a metaphor is produced in which "terror" becomes the opposing army. As in any war, the enemy must be defeated. But "terror" is not actually an army—it is a state of mind. As such, it cannot be beaten on a field of battle. It is an emotion. Moreover, the "war on terror" frame is self-perpetuating; merely being in a war scares citizens, and reiteration of the frame creates more fear. So there is no end to the "war on terror," because you can't permanently capture and defeat an emotion.

A strategic advantage of the frame is that "war" also invokes Article II of the Constitution, giving the president broad powers as commander in chief. It allows the military to perform what is essentially a police function: bringing criminals to justice. It negates due process, because in war you assume the enemy is guilty—you shoot to kill.

This is a powerful surface frame, with a wide-reaching set of implications. So why did the "war on terror" phrase resonate, given how misleading it is? Why does it persist to this day?

It works because it relies on conservative *deep frames*. When something "resonates" or "makes sense," it engages your deep frames. Conservatives have long advanced the idea that our military can—and should—be used to shape foreign policy; our *strength* is the size and capacity of our military. They have advanced a retributive crime policy—punish the wrongdoers, no need to look at systemic causes of crime. The "war on terror" activates these deep frames, and politicians, the media, and the public continue to use the phrase because the conservative deep frames have become so pervasive.

If *progressive* deep frames had been articulated and present in the public mind, the idea of a "war on terror" never would have made sense. If we viewed our *strength* as our diplomatic ability to forge international consensus and coalitions, and if we recognized that killing and maiming civilians through military action creates more terrorists and fosters more acts of terrorism, we wouldn't have looked to our military to solve the problem. Had progressive deep frames been prevalent at the time of 9/11, Americans would have taken "war on terror" as a powerful metaphor but not a literal guide to action, like the "war on poverty." They would have seen it as a major crime problem— like international organized crime—and sought to bring these criminals to justice by the means that work best, like tracing bank accounts, placing spies in their organizations, and so on.

It is difficult to overemphasize the importance of deep framing—the framing of moral values and principles. It is a long-term enterprise and entirely different from crafting short-term messages about a single issue or candidate that use surface frames, and it is more important. Without the long-term deep frames in place, the short-term slogans have no structure to build upon. They don't resonate because they don't reinforce any deep frames. (One of the most frustrating experiences of the Rockridge staff is when we are asked to help craft a message on a single issue for an advocacy or grassroots group. It is hard to explain that slogans or phrases in a value vacuum don't do much good.)

So how are deep frames embedded in the public mind? To cultivate new deep frames requires going on the offense with your values and principles, repeating them over and over and over. It cannot be done through a single ad campaign or a single group or a single election. It cannot work as part of a "war room," or a "rapid response" approach, which is inherently reactive, not proactive. It must be done over a long period, planned in advance and perhaps as a part of many short-term campaigns. And it must be done by many organizations working in concert across issue areas.

For more discussion of surface frames—like "tax relief"—you can read *Don't Think of an Elephant!* or go to our Web site, www.rockridgeinstitute.org.

ISSUE-DEFINING FRAMES: IRAQ AND IMMIGRATION

Just as frames structure and define social institutions, they also define issues. An issue-defining frame characterizes the problem, assigns blame, and constrains the possible solutions. More important, issue-defining frames *block* relevant concerns if those concerns are outside of the frame.

Issue-defining frames exist at an intermediate depth, between the surface frames that conceptualize slogans about issues and the deep frames, those for values, principles, and fundamental concepts that go across issues.

For a current example of an issue-defining frame, let's look at Iraq. Conservatives have taken the framing initiative and continue to call it "war." This frame has very real implications, especially considering the commonplace theory that America fights only the good fight. If what is happening in Iraq is seen as a "war," it has to be a just war, despite how and why we got into it. It has to be a war against evil, or we wouldn't be in it. And we have to fight to the finish, however difficult it may be.

In the "war" frame, "cut and run"—a typically conservative response to reasonable proposals of withdrawing troops, or setting a timetable, or, at the least, setting goals in Iraq—applies. Here's the conceptual frame associated with "cut and run":

> There is a war being fought against evil. Fighting requires courage and bravery. Those fully committed to the cause are brave. Those who "cut and run" are interested only in saving their own skins, not in the moral cause; they are cowards. The "cut and run" approach endangers both the moral cause and the lives of the brave troops who are fighting for it. Those with courage and conviction stand and fight.

The "war" frame not only defines what's happening in Iraq but also constrains the solutions. In a war, it is cowardly and immoral to "cut and run."

The "war" frame is a trap, and those opposed to "staying the course" have repeatedly fallen in. John Murtha responded to the "cut and run" accusation with "stay and pay," and John Kerry with "lie and die." Senator Jack Reed suggested "the plan to be in Iraq forever."

What's wrong with these responses? First, the grammar— X and Y—evokes the "cut and run" frame and thus reinforces it. Then, each one of these is a self-interest, save-our-skins frame that accepts the "war" frame and says it is in our interest to get out. We "pay," we "die," we are stuck there forever. This does not reject the "cut and run" frame, which presupposes a war against evil. It accepts that frame and takes the saving-our-skin position, which in the frame is cowardly and immoral. The advocates of removing our troops fell right into the trap.

The war frame is dishonest and has led to a tragic loss of life. We need to reframe what's going on in Iraq and tell the truth: *This is an occupation, not a war.*

Notice how the "occupation" frame—as an issue-defining frame—restructures the terms of the debate to illuminate more honest concerns. In an occupation, there are pragmatic issues: Are we welcome? Are we doing the Iraqis more harm than good? How badly are we being hurt? The question is not *whether* to withdraw but *when*. In an occupation, the problem is not an evil enemy. The problem is when to leave. The solutions that "make sense" in an occupation are entirely different from the solutions that "make sense" in a war.

Further, the occupation frame is more *honest*. The war was over when Bush famously stood on the aircraft carrier in front of a "Mission Accomplished" banner and announced the end of major military operations. A war has one army fighting another army over territory. Our fighting men and women defeated Saddam's military machine shortly after the invasion in March 2003. Then came the occupation. Our troops were trained to fight a war, not to occupy a country where they don't know the language and culture, where they don't have enough troops, where they face an anti-occupation insurgency by the Iraqis themselves, where there is a civil war going on, and where most Iraqis want them out.

For another illustrative issue-defining frame, let's turn to immigration. Here, conservatives again took the initiative and defined the problem as "illegal immigration." The roles in this frame are the immigrants and American agencies concerned with immigration (under the Department of Homeland Security). The principal cause of the problem is the immigrants, and the secondary cause is the inability of the agencies to stop the immigrants from crossing the border.

Under such framing, the immigrants have committed the crime of crossing the border and are seen as felons; by "taking jobs from Americans" and making use of social services, they are putting a strain on local governments and "taking money out of taxpayers' pockets." Possible "solutions" flow from that framing: rounding up immigrants and deporting them; granting citizenship to those here longest and deporting those here less than two years; instituting a "temporary worker" program to legally admit workers here for a short time, denying them many basic rights and any hope of citizenship.

Such framing overlooks many concerns of progressives, such as the essential work undocumented immigrants perform, the basic denial of civil rights, the trade policies that have forced people into unemployment in Mexico, or the way our economy drives wages down to the lowest possible level.

Let's see what happens if we reframe the issue and define it as a problem of "illegal employers." Now the problem becomes the employers who are hiring undocumented workers so they can pay workers less or skirt paying taxes. Employers are recognized as driving down wages, hurting American workers, and exploiting immigrants, many of whom have already fled oppressive circumstances.

The possible solutions that flow from such framing are much different: Fine or punish employers for hiring undocumented workers or provide a way for these workers to get the proper documents and work with due protection of the law. This is a way to unite immigrants and American workers, ensuring that all have access to decent wages, rather than dividing them—by pitting their interests against one another—and overlooking the system that drives down all of their wages.

There are other ways of framing the issue that focus on progressive values. An "immigrant gratitude" frame, which honors their contributions and compensates them with necessary social services and a reasonable path to citizenship. A "cheap labor" frame, which focuses on the forces in the economy that are really hurting American workers—seeing labor not as an asset but as a resource whose cost must be minimized if profits are to be maximized. A "creating immigrants" frame that focuses on what causes people to flee their homes and come to the United States—poverty and/or political oppression in their native country and, in certain cases, American trade policy that impoverishes people elsewhere. Any solution would require a reevaluation of our foreign policy toward such nations and our "free-trade" policies.[5]

What these exercises show is simple: Frames not only define issues, problems, causes, and solutions; they also hide relevant issues and causes. Moreover, policies and programs make sense only given issue-defining frames.

MESSAGING FRAMES

Among the many kind of frames—besides surface frames, deep frames, and issue-defining frames—are messaging frames, familiar to media scholars. There are many genres, and each has its own rules: political speeches and debates, advertising, news stories, editorials, and commentaries. What they have in common are certain semantic roles: messengers, audience, issue, message, medium, and images.

Crucial to the message is the *messenger*. In the 2005 campaign in California's special election, the most effective messengers against Governor Arnold Schwarzenegger's proposals to reshape state government were nurses and firefighters. They had integrity and credibility.

As a messenger, George W. Bush is remarkably aware of his *audience* and often includes hidden messages to his base. *Props* matter. To appear folksy, Bush releases images of himself using his chain saw on his ranch. The *medium*—radio, TV, newspapers—makes an enormous difference. On TV, images are more important than words. In print ads, what comes first is usually more important than later text.

LESSONS FROM COGNITIVE SCIENCE

1. The use of frames is largely unconscious. The use of frames occurs at the neural level, so most people have no idea they are even using frames, much less what kind of frames. Thus, the conservative message machine can impose its frames without the public—progressive or not—being aware of them. For example, the "war on terror" frame has been imposed by conservatives but used by independent journalists and even by many progressives without much comment. In another area, *Time* magazine ran the headline "Illegals!" for a feature article on immigration. Democrats have used the "tax relief" frame without being aware that it undercuts their own views.

2. Frames define common sense. What counts as "common sense" varies from person to person but always depends on what frames are in the brain and how frequently they are used and evoked. Different people can have different frames in their brains, so "common sense" can differ widely from person to person. However, in getting their frames to dominate public discourse, conservatives have changed "common sense," and progressives have been letting them get away with it. Progressives should become conscious of framing that is at present accepted unconsciously as "common sense" but that hides the deep problems.

3. Repetition can embed frames in the brain. One of the funniest bits on Jon Stewart's *The Daily Show* is video clips it runs of right-wing leaders and spokespeople using the same words over and over on the same day. The technique of repetition of the same words to express the same idea is effective. The words come with surface frames. Those surface frames in turn latch onto and activate deep frames. When repeated over and over, the words reinforce deep frames by strengthening neural connections in listeners.

4. Activation links surface frames to deep frames and inhibits opposition frames. When the surface frames are activated, the deep frames that make sense of them are activated as well. The activation of conservative deep frames—the conservative moral system and the political and economic principles that follow from that—then inhibits the progressive moral system and principles.

5. Existing deep frames don't change overnight. Brains don't change quickly. Just using your own language, with your surface framing, won't necessarily convince people. Your deep framing must be established in order for your surface frames to have any effect. Persistence is key!

6. Speak to biconceptuals as you speak to your base. The brain permits different—and inconsistent—moral worldviews to govern different aspects of one's life. The morality that governs your life Saturday night in the club might not be the same one that governs your behavior the next morning in church. In politics, we use the term "swing voters" for biconceptuals who can apply either a progressive or a conservative moral worldview to politics. Another way to put this is that either worldview—either set of deep frames—can be activated when making political decisions.

Conservatives seek to activate conservative deep frames in biconceptuals by activating conservative surface frames linked to those deep frames. As we have observed, they speak to the center by speaking to their base. Progressives should do the same. When progressives "move to the right" by adopting conservative positions, they activate and reinforce conservative deep frames—conservative values and positions.

7. The facts alone will not set you free. Facts can be assimilated into the brain only if there is a frame to make sense out of them. We think and reason using frames and metaphors. The consequence is that arguing simply in terms of facts—how many people have no health insurance, how many degrees Earth has warmed in the last decade, how long it's been since the last raise in the minimum wage—will likely fall on deaf ears. That's not to say the facts aren't important. They are *extremely* important. But they make sense only given a context.

8. Simply negating the other side's frames only reinforces them. The title of the book *Don't Think of an Elephant!* says it all: Tell someone that, and he or she *will* think of an elephant. Like every other word, "elephant" is defined by a frame that contains a mental image of an elephant and some crucial information about elephants: They have trunks, huge round bodies, big floppy ears, and so on. The word evokes the frame, even if you ask someone not to think of an elephant. When former president Richard Nixon spoke his famous line, "I am not a crook," *everyone thought of him as a crook.* When Senator Joe Lieberman said "I am not George Bush" in a debate with Ned Lamont, *everyone thought of him as George Bush.*

There are limited cases where the use of the other side's frames can be effective. For example, you might be skillful enough to undermine one of their frames by following its inferences to a logically absurd conclusion. When Republicans presented the "Contract with America" in 1994, one Democratic response was to warn people to "read the fine print."

THE PROBLEM OF RATIONALISM

Understanding frame analysis means becoming aware of one's own mind and the minds of others. This is a big task. We were not brought up to think in terms of frames and metaphors and moral worldviews. We *were* brought up to believe that there is only one common sense and that it is the same for everyone. Not true. Our common sense is determined by the frames we unconsciously acquire, and one person's common sense is another's evil political ideology. The truths that have been discovered about the mind are not easy to fathom, especially when false views of the mind get in the way.

The discovery of frames requires a reevaluation of rationalism, a 350-year-old theory of mind that arose during the Enlightenment. We say this with great admiration for the rationalist tradition. It is rationalism, after all, that provided the foundation for our democratic system. Rationalism says it is reason that makes us human, and all human beings are equally rational. That is why we can govern ourselves and do not have to rely upon a king or a pope to govern us. And since we are equally rational, the best form of government is a democracy. So far, so good.

But rationalism also comes with several false theories of mind.

- We know from cognitive science research that most thought is unconscious, but rationalism claims that all thought is conscious.
- We know that we think using mechanisms like frames

and metaphors. Yet rationalism claims that all thought is literal, that it can directly fit the world; this rules out any effects of framing, metaphors, and worldviews.

- We know that people with different worldviews think differently and may reach completely different conclusions given the same facts. But rationalism claims that we all have the same universal reason. Some aspects of reason *are* universal, but many others are not—they differ from person to person based on their worldview and deep frames.

- We know that people reason using the logic of frames and metaphors, which falls outside of classical logic. But rationalism assumes that thought is logical and fits classical logic.

Rationalism says that people vote on the basis of their material self-interest, that they are conscious of why they voted, that they can tell a pollster what their most important concerns are, and that they will vote for the candidate who best addresses those concerns.

But we know from Wirthlin (see Chapter 1) that this is false. The rationalist theory of voters isn't true. Yet progressive pollsters still act as if it is. And progressive candidates take their advice. They run on a laundry list of programs recommended by their pollsters and act as if Wirthlin had never made his discovery.

If you believed in rationalism, you would believe that *the facts will set you free*, that you just need to give people hard information, independent of any framing, and they will reason their way to the right conclusion. We know this is false, that if the facts don't fit the frames people have, they will keep the frames (which are, after all, physically in their brains) and ignore, forget, or explain away the facts. The facts must be framed in a way to make sense in order to be accepted as a basis for further reasoning.

If you were a rationalist policy maker, you would believe that frames, metaphors, and moral worldviews played no role in characterizing problems or solutions to problems. You would believe that all problems and solutions were objective and in no way worldview dependent. You would believe that solutions were rational, and that the tools to be used in arriving at them included classical logic, probability theory, game theory, cost-benefit analysis, and other aspects of the theory of rational action.

You would further believe in the classical theory of categories, and you would divide up the policy-making world by categories, creating issue "silos." Thus, there would be educational policies, separate from health policies, separate from environmental policies, and so on.

Rationalism pervades the progressive world. It is one of the reasons progressives have lately been losing to conservatives.

Rationalist-based political campaigns miss the symbolic, metaphorical, moral, emotional, and frame-based aspects of political campaigns. *Real* rationality recognizes these politically crucial aspects of our mental life. We advocate getting real about rationality itself, recognizing how it really works. If you think political campaigns are about laundry lists of policies that have no further symbolic value, then you miss the heart of American politics.

EXPRESSING OUR VALUES

To get out of the rationalist trap, progressives must understand their deepest implicit values and make them explicit. But this is a bit tricky.

Progressive candidates have been having a problem telling the public what they stand for. They have difficulties expressing their values and their political principles. Yet progressives *do* stand for something (usually a lot) and *do* have values and political principles. Why can't they just say what they are? If you can't tell me what you stand for, it sounds like you don't stand for anything. What is going on here? How can intelligent, articulate people in public life stand for something without being able to say what they stand for?

The answer is simple from a cognitive science point of view. Our conceptual systems are unconscious. We usually cannot directly access unconscious systems of ideas. The result is that progressives tend to "feel" when a proposed policy sounds like the right—or wrong—thing to do. But many progressives cannot say exactly *why* they feel as they do, exactly what moral principles make it the right—or wrong—thing to do.

So progressives tend to find it difficult to provide morally based arguments for positions that they think are right. We hope, through this handbook, to begin to make the implicit reasons explicit—to fill in the gaps in progressive forms of argument—and to help progressives express the moral values and principles they really believe in.

FRAME OR LOSE

Lately, one school of thought making the rounds among progressives is that it may be best not to engage in articulating our values and principles, and not to do much of anything to put forth a progressive vision. The thinking, in a nutshell, is that things are going so wrong for conservatives that they are likely to self-destruct.

This is a terrible mistake. One thing we know about how brains change is that they can change more radically under conditions of trauma than under ordinary conditions. The questions are: What will the direction of the change be? How will the trauma or other disaster be framed? And who will get to frame it?

If progressives say nothing when disaster occurs from conservative policies, then conservatives will get to frame the disasters—and they will certainly *not* frame them as failures of conservative philosophy. They may twist the nature of causation and blame the disaster on progressives.

Failing that, there are other ways out. Consider, for instance, the various responses to crises that have come from the Bush administration: *It was a failure of intelligence. It was an honest mistake. There were tactical errors. No one could have guessed it would happen. Everyone has made sacrifices and done the best anyone could expect of them. There were a few bad apples, and we're taking care of them.* They could admit incompetence and replace the incompetent persons with people who look more competent. Or they could even argue that they were not conservative enough, reframing the disaster for still more conservative ends. When there is a loud, powerful, and effective chorus of progressive voices heard, conservatives can't use their effective reframing machine to snatch victory from the jaws of defeat. That is why we cannot be silent.

When conservative philosophy causes disaster, progressives must make that clear, shout it from the rooftops, organize speakers everywhere to say it out loud, and repeat it until it registers in the brains of the public and becomes *an issue*, a matter of ongoing public debate. When there are victims, conservative villains, and progressive heroes, it should be made clear who is who.[6]

REFRAMING: WORDS TO RECLAIM

Conservatives have worked hard to redefine our words—that is, change the frame associated with a word so that it fits the conservative worldview. In so doing, they have changed the meaning of some of our most important concepts and have stolen our language.

Most notably, they have redefined the word "liberal." They have turned it upside down. What once was—and still should be—a badge of pride is now a label to run from. Consider the differences between the conservative tag on "liberal" and the real meaning that we should hold near and dear to our hearts.

Conservatives: Tax-and-spend liberals want to take your hard-earned money and give it to lazy no-accounts. Latte-sipping liberals are elitists who look down their noses at you. Hollywood liberals have no family values. The liberal media twist the facts. Leftist liberals want to end the free market. Antiwar liberals are unpatriotic wimps who can't defend our country. Secular liberals want to end religion.

Liberals: Liberty-loving liberals founded our country and enshrined its freedoms. Dedicated, fair-minded liberals ended slavery and brought women the vote. Hardworking liberals fought the goon squads and won workers' rights: the eight-hour day, the weekend, health plans, and pensions. Courageous liberals risked their lives to win civil rights. Caring liberals have made the vulnerable elderly secure with Social Security and healthy with Medicare. Forward-looking liberals have extended education to everyone. Liberals who love the land have been preserving our environment so you can enjoy it. Nobody loves liberty and life more than a liberal. When conservatives say you're on your own, we liberals know we're all in this together.

"Liberal" is not the only example of the right's framing larceny. Here are other examples of words worth reclaiming—and how conservatives and progressives view them.

PATRIOTISM

Conservatives: Patriots do not question the president or his war policies. To do so undermines our nation and its troops. Revealing secret, even illegal, government programs is treasonous. The Constitution should be amended to criminalize political dissent in the form of flag desecration.

Progressives: The greatest testament to one's love of country is when one works to improve it. This includes principled dissent against policies one disagrees with and against leaders who promote those policies. Times of war are no exception. Our first loyalty is to the principles of our democracy that are embedded in our Constitution, not to any political leader.

RULE OF LAW

Conservatives: Criminals deserve strict punishment for their crimes. If that means two million people are in U.S. prisons, so be it. If police have to step on a few toes or cross a few constitutional lines, so be it. Courts have gone too far in letting criminals go free on "technicalities." Strict sentencing constraints should overrule any tendency toward leniency on the part of judge or jury. As commander in chief, the president is the highest authority. He may choose not to observe domestic and international laws when he deems it necessary to fight our enemies. Some civil liberties are also subordinate to this fight.

Progressives: No one is above the law. The president must abide by constitutional limitations on his power and follow laws passed by Congress; police and judges must respect the constitutional rights of all citizens. Criminals must be accountable for their crimes, but society should temper its desire for retribution with wisdom and compassion. In civil matters, access to the courts should be equally available to all. Corporations and individuals must be accountable for injuries they inflict. The United States must abide by international law and treaty obligations.

NATIONAL SECURITY

Conservatives: It's a scary world. Fanatics wish us harm. We must respond with every means available to us, including torture and indefinite imprisonment without trial of those we suspect of acting against us. We must take the fight to the enemy regardless of the cost in lives, dollars, strained alliances, and our international reputation. Military force is our greatest weapon.

Progressives: It's a scary world, but for reasons that go well beyond the threat of terror. We can deal with terrorism far more wisely and without invading foreign nations under false pretenses. Terrorism is an international problem; we can fight it more effectively in partnership with other nations than by going it alone. We should fight terrorism with the tools for fighting international organized crime, rather than with the military. Moreover, we must recognize that our long-term security is also threatened by climate destabilization and pollution, by our dependence on foreign energy, by the growing gap between rich and poor, and by our faltering public education system.

FAMILY VALUES

Conservatives: Obedience and discipline are the core values of the family. Sex education in the schools, the right to abortion, and gay marriage undermine obedience and discipline. They are an affront to the family.

Progressives: Empathy and responsibility for oneself and others are the core values of the family. Respectful, loving, and supportive parenting promotes healthy families. Health care, education, food on the table, and social systems are essential to the well-being of the family. Loving, committed, and supportive individuals define the family, not gender roles.

LIFE

Conservatives: Abortion is the immoral taking of innocent life. It must be banned.

Progressives: Promoting life means ending America's huge infant mortality rate through pre- and postnatal care. It means caring for individuals throughout their lives. It means affordable universal health care to improve life and life expectancy for forty-five million uninsured Americans. It means improving the quality of the air we breathe and the water we drink. It means improving schools and parenting so that every young life has a chance to flower. It means finding ways to end the violence in our society that cuts short so many lives. It means fulfilling the promise of stem cell research, rather than destroying the hopes of millions of suffering Americans for the sake of a tiny cluster of undifferentiated cells that will otherwise be discarded.

Taking back these and other words is a long-term enterprise. The right didn't snatch them overnight, and we can't take them back quickly, either. But they can be reclaimed. They must be spoken often. And they must be spoken in the contexts in which progressives understand them.

Consider progressives across the country consistently saying something like this: "I am for life. That's why I support the right of all women to receive prenatal care and the right of all children to receive immunizations and to be treated when they are sick. That's why I believe we must safeguard the planet that sustains all life."

Or perhaps this: "I am a patriot. That's why I am compelled to oppose the government's spying on American citizens without court order and in defiance of Congress."

Repetition of such articulations is the key to redefining these words and reclaiming them. Progressives must say things like this when they speak to their friends, when they write letters to the editor, when they blog, when they run for office. Once this process begins, continues, and is repeated often enough, these words and the public's understanding of them can return to their traditional meanings. It will not be easy, but it must be done.

,

4

THE NATION AS FAMILY

It's no accident that our political beliefs are structured by our idealizations of the family. Our earliest experience with being governed is in our families. Our parents "govern" us: They protect us, tell us what we can and cannot do, make sure we have enough money and supplies, educate us, and have us do our part in running the house.

So it is not at all surprising that many nations are metaphorically seen in terms of families: *Mother* Russia, *Mother* India, the *Father*land. In America, we have founding *fathers, Daughters* of the American Revolution, *Uncle* Sam, and we send our collective *sons and daughters* to war. In George Orwell's dystopian novel *1984*, the voice of the totalitarian state was called *Big Brother*.

As George Lakoff discussed at length in his 1996 book, *Moral Politics*, this metaphorical understanding of the nation-as-family directly informs our political worldview.[1] Directly, but not consciously. As with other aspects of framing, the use of this metaphor lies below the level of consciousness. But unlike other, more modest framings, the nation-as-family metaphor structures entire worldviews, organizing whole systems of frames in our brains. This was an empirical discovery about how people think about politics. Using cognitive modeling and the cognitive theory of metaphor (see *Moral Politics* for methodological details), Lakoff formulated the nation-as-family metaphor as a precise mapping between the nation and the family: the homeland as home, the citizens as siblings, the government (or the head of government) as parent. The government's duty is to citizens as a parent's is to children: provide security (protect us); make laws (tell us what we can and cannot do); run the economy (make sure we have enough money and supplies); provide public schools (educate us).

This metaphor explains many of the profound differences between pure progressives and pure conservatives on all sorts of issues—from abortion to gun control, from environmental regulation to lawsuit restrictions, from "gay marriage" to the estate tax. Why? Simply put, Americans have two very different idealized models of the family: a "strict father" family and a "nurturant parent" family. This produces two fundamentally opposed moral systems for running a nation—two ideologies that specify not only how the nation should be governed but also, in many respects, how we should live our lives.

But we are all biconceptuals; both models are seared into our brains. Each may be used actively (in politics or everyday life) or passively (say, in understanding movies). The models are *cultural*, and, by virtue of living in the same culture, we become familiar with both models.

Being conservative in some aspect of life, say, religion, means that you use a strict father model to govern your functioning in that arena. Similarly, being progressive in some aspect of life means that you use a nurturant parent model to understand and function in that arena. Pure conservatives and pure liberals use one model to govern all aspects of their political life.

The two models contradict each other; they cannot be applied in the same situation at the same time by the same person. In neural terms, they are mutually inhibitory: activating one inhibits the other.

This is the *Moral Politics* model. It is a theoretical construct within cognitive science that explains many aspects of American political life.

It also explains the nature of ideological purity—why pure conservatives are anti-abortion, anti–gun control, for "tort reform," against environmental regulation, for lower taxes, against "gay marriage," and so on, while pure progressives have the opposite views. The *Moral Politics* model explicates the political visions of pure progressives and conservatives and the modes of reasoning characteristic of both.

The model also illuminates a very important political phenomenon. Why do fundamentalist Christians tend to be right-wing conservatives rather than progressives? For instance, why is James Dobson of Focus on the Family, a child-rearing educator from the Christian Coalition, a powerful force in right-wing politics? Dobson is a major proponent of the strict father family in actual family life.[2] Why is he a right-wing conservative rather than a progressive? The *Moral Politics* model explains why.

Fundamentalist Christians view God as a strict father, and the model that structures their religion and their family life also structures their politics. As we will see in Chapter 6, conservatives and progressives differ on the meaning of our most fundamental political concepts: fairness, freedom, equality, responsibility, integrity, and security. The strict/nurturant distinction in family models predicts these differences in the meaning of our most central political concepts.

It is crucial to distinguish between mental models and the names we use for them. Naming is an inexact art. In general, simple names cannot accurately characterize the richness of the models. For example, the strict father model refers to the strictness of the father in applying punishment to a misbehaving child. But the model is far richer than that. The term "strict father" does not capture the focus on the "free" market, the focus on individual discipline, and many other aspects of conservative politics.

The same is true of the nurturant parent model. "Nurturance" characterizes the empathy and care aspects of the model, but the name is less clear about the responsibility aspect, the strength needed for responsibility, and the implications about protection, freedom, fairness, and so on.

Many other names for these models have been tried, but the inherent limitations on naming will always lead to a discrepancy between the name and model.

THE NURTURANT PARENT MODEL

In this model, if there are two parents, both are equally responsible for the moral development of the children. Their primary duty is to love their children and nurture them to be happy in their lives. Nurturing has two aspects: empathy and responsibility, both for oneself and for others. Remember that to take care of others, you have to take care of yourself. Equally important, parents raise their children to nurture others, which requires children to have empathy for others, responsibility for oneself, and social responsibility. This is the very opposite of indulgence or spoiling.

Nurturant parents are *authoritative* without being *authoritarian*. They set fair and reasonable limits and rules, and take the trouble to discuss them with their children. Obedience derives from love for parents, not from fear of punishment. Open and respectful communication takes place between parents and children. Parents explain their decisions in order to legitimize their authority. Parents accept questioning by children as a positive trait but reserve the ultimate decision making for themselves.

Parents protect their children from external threats as a natural expression of their love and care.

THE PROGRESSIVE VISION

Apply the nurturant parent model to politics, and what you get is progressive moral and political philosophy. Though progressive thought can be extremely complex when one gets into the details, it is actually quite simple at the highest level of moral values and general principles.[3]

Progressive morality, like the nurturant parent model, is based on *empathy* and *responsibility*.

Empathy is the capacity to connect with other people, to feel what others feel, to imagine oneself as another and hence to feel a kinship with others.

Responsibility means acting on that empathy—responsibility for yourself and for others.

From empathy and responsibility, a set of core progressive values follows. These are the values that define progressive thought and structure progressive positions on any issue. They all involve *acting on your empathy* to achieve the following:

- *Protection* (for people threatened or under duress)
- *Fulfillment in life* (so others can lead meaningful lives as you would want to)
- *Freedom* (because to seek fulfillment, you must be free)
- *Opportunity* (because leading a fulfilling life requires opportunities to explore what is meaningful and fruitful)
- *Fairness* (because unfairness can stifle freedom and opportunity)
- *Equality* (because empathy extends to everyone)
- *Prosperity* (because a certain base amount of material wealth is necessary to lead a fulfilling life and pay for enough shelter, food, and health)
- *Community* (because nobody makes it alone, and communities are necessary for anyone to lead a fulfilling life)

Remember that you have to take care of yourself if you are to act responsibly toward others. In progressive morality, there is no contradiction between acting to take care of yourself and acting to help others, since you can't take care of others if you are not taking care of yourself. The old dichotomy between self-interest and altruism is false, since extreme self-sacrifice can make it impossible to act for the sake of others.

Naturally flowing from these progressive values are four core political principles. These principles, largely unconscious, are found over and over again as the basis of arguments for progressive policies and programs.

The Common Good Principle

Franklin Roosevelt said in his second inaugural address, "In our personal ambitions we are individualists. But in our seeking for economic and political progress as a nation, we all go up, or else we all go down, as one people." In short, the common good is necessary for individual well-being. Citizens bring together their common wealth for the common good in order to build an infrastructure that benefits all and that contributes crucially to the pursuit of individual goals. (Warren Buffett has famously observed that he could not have achieved his wealth had he lived in Bangladesh, where the banking system and stock market leave much to be desired.[4])

Here are a few things that taxpayer money—the common wealth—pays for: the interstate highway system, the satellite system, the security system (police, firefighters, the military), the banking system, the court system. Just about every business depends on bank loans (the banking system), contract enforcement (the court system), communications (the Internet and satellite systems), and the shipping of goods (the highway system).

The common wealth provides *protection* for the common good: police, military, firefighters, courts.

It allows for *fulfillment in life* and creates *opportunities*, thereby enhancing the common good: schools, universities, national parks, roads, a banking infrastructure to start a business. The more money one makes, the more one tends to use the common wealth, and the more responsibility one has to contribute to its maintenance. That is an important moral basis for progressive taxation.

The common wealth creates *freedoms* for the common good. Freedom is enshrined in our Constitution, is protected by the courts, and is enhanced by the common wealth. The social safety net and Social Security grant us *freedom from want*. The Bill of Rights grants us a host of other freedoms.

The common good principle promotes *fairness* and *equality*. A progressive government guards against discrimination and works to prevent underserved communities. It operates on the principle that *we're all in this together*, not that you're on your own. Being in this together means that we get the benefits of everyone working for the common good, as well as the responsibilities.

Using the common wealth for the common good creates *prosperity* and fosters *community*.

In business, the common good principle results in ethical business practices. An ethical business does no harm—to individuals, communities, or the environment. It also contributes real benefits to the public as well as its employees and its community. A progressive government acts to support ethical business and to discourage, or even prosecute, unethical business.

The common good principle also means the preservation of common property, or the commons: national monuments; public parks and beaches; the oceans, rivers, and streams; the electromagnetic spectrum (used for radio, TV, and other forms of communication); scientific knowledge; our genetic heritage; and the Internet. These serve us all, and they must be kept public for future generations.

The Expansion of Freedom Principle

Progressive moral values lead—and have historically led—Americans to demand the expansion of fundamental forms of freedom. They include voting rights, workers' rights, public education, public health, consumer protection, civil rights, and civil liberties. These expansions reveal what traditional American values have been about.[5]

The Human Dignity Principle

Empathy requires the recognition of basic human dignity, and responsibility requires us to act to uphold it.

This principle provides baselines for a wide range of progressive arguments: against torture, for intervention to prevent genocide, for programs to meet the basic needs of the poor, for women's rights, against racism, and so on.

As a country, we need to decide where the boundary of human dignity falls. Food, shelter, education, and health care are all basic rights for all people. Progressives, acting on their belief in human dignity, feel it is necessary to secure these rights for all our citizens.

The Diversity Principle

Empathy—which involves identifying with and connecting socially and emotionally with the other—leads to an ethic of diversity in our communities, schools, and workplaces. Diversity fosters meaningful *communities* and creates a range of *opportunities* for citizens to lead *fulfilling lives*.

"Diversity" has become a progressive code word for measures against the effects of discrimination on the basis of race, ethnicity, religion, gender, and sexual preference. Because these forms of discrimination have been so widespread and their effects so long-lasting, they have reduced the possibilities for societal enrichment through diversity.

Market diversity, say, in energy or agriculture, provides *protec-*

tion, so that a shortage in one area can easily be dealt with by surplus or production in another. If we have access to a diversity of energy sources, we will not be susceptible to the difficult consequences of rising oil and gas prices. Biological diversity both guarantees against monocultures being wiped out by some pestilence and serves to promote appreciation of the wonders of nature. Artistic and musical diversity allows for the creation of new forms of art and music.

We will now take a look at the competing "strict father" model and the very different set of guiding values and principles that flow from it.

THE STRICT FATHER MODEL

A family has two parents, a father and a mother. We live in a dangerous world, where there is constant competition with inevitable winners and losers. The family requires a strong father to protect it from the many evils in the world and to support it by winning those competitions.

Morally, there are absolute rights and wrongs. The strict father is the moral authority in the family; he knows right from wrong, is inherently moral, and heads the household. The father's authority and decisions are not to be challenged. Obedience to the father is moral; disobedience is immoral.

The mother supports and upholds the authority of the father but is not strong enough to protect the family or to impose moral order by herself. She provides affection to the children to show love, reward right conduct, and provide comfort in the face of punishment.

Children are born undisciplined. The father teaches them

discipline and right from wrong. When children disobey, the father is obligated to punish, providing an incentive to avoid punishment and helping his children develop the internal discipline to do right. This "tough love" is seen as the only way to teach morality. Children who are disciplined enough to be moral can also use that discipline as adults to seek their self-interest in the market and become prosperous.

Again, that is the ideal model. In real families, it is commonplace to have, say, a strict father and a nurturant mother. Siblings may identify with different parents and grow up with different ideal models.

Pure conservative philosophy is the application of the strict father model—and only that model—to politics. Many self-identified "conservative" voices have actually been biconceptuals of various sorts, e.g., economically conservative but progressive about civil liberties, economically progressive but socially conservative, or vice versa. Such divisions among partial conservatives defined the old fault lines within the conservative movement: libertarians, fiscal conservatives, social conservatives, religious fundamentalists, and more recently, neoconservatives.

What is relatively new in American conservative politics is the attempt to weed the partial progressives out of leadership positions so that pure conservatives are left as the dominant leaders, applying the strict father model to *all* issue areas.

Also new is the appearance of the *authoritarian conservative*, who applies the strict father model not just to all issues but to *governing itself*! The George W. Bush administration has placed itself above Congress (choosing which parts of which laws it will accept) and above the courts (fighting to avoid jurisdiction). Bush himself has been governing as the ultimate moral authority—the decider—not only in the administration but in the Republican caucuses in Congress, in the Republican Party itself, and even in much of the conservative media. A great many old-guard conservatives were *not* authoritarians in their own community or in governing the nation. John W. Dean, for example, a Goldwater conservative who worked in the administration of former president Richard M. Nixon, considers the Bush administration so authoritarian as to border on fascism.[6]

THE CONSERVATIVE VISION

Conservative morality centers on issues of *authority* and *control*, both self-control (discipline) and control over others.

Authority should be legitimate and morally good. Authorities have power and, since they are inherently good, use it legitimately to exert control. A political authority has been elected or chosen and thus has legitimate moral authority, which must be respected.

Other values follow from these fundamental components of authority and control:

Discipline: Self-control is an essential quality. Moral authority requires internal discipline, which is learned through punishment when one does wrong. The failure of an authority to punish for wrongdoing is a moral failure.

There are political consequences of such a view. Getting something one hasn't earned weakens one's discipline and hence one's capacity to be moral. Thus, if you are not prosperous, you are not disciplined enough to be prosperous and therefore deserve your poverty. Social programs, which give people things they haven't earned, lessen people's incentive to be disciplined and, hence, to be moral. Social programs thus serve immorality and should be abandoned.

Ownership: Property acquired through a market or other legitimate means is yours to do with as you see fit. You can spend your money better than the government can. The only use of the common wealth for the common good is to provide *physical security*. The profit motive creates efficiency in business. Government, lacking a profit motive, is inefficient and wasteful—and gets in the way of the market via regulation, taxation, unionization, and lawsuits.

Hierarchy: Economic, social, and political hierarchy is natural because some people are more talented and disciplined than others and deserve to be higher on the totem pole. This is *equity*—higher position earned through merit (talent and discipline)—not equality. Equality of opportunity produces a hierarchy based on merit. And because the market is seen as natural and fair and as allowing the cream to rise to the top, success is an indicator of merit. This directly links democracy to a meritocracy.

Conservative philosophy does not recognize any of the progressive principles. For instance, the "common good principle" is seen as interfering with the free market, the system that rewards discipline. The freedoms that progressives want to expand—particularly freedom from want—are not seen as "freedoms" by conservatives. The "human dignity principle" is rejected by most conservatives because they believe humans do not have an inalienable dignity but must prove their self-worth through self-discipline. If they cannot provide for themselves, too bad. There are exceptions: God-fearing, churchgoing, hardworking people with conservative family values are the "worthy poor," deserving of private charity. But "worth" is not conferred on just anybody by virtue of being human.

Finally, the "diversity principle" is not valued for its own sake—it is overridden by a merit-based market that confers success through competition.

In contrast to the progressive principles, conservatives have the following:

The Moral Authority Principle

Morality comes from obeying legitimate moral authorities: God (or His minister or priest), the law, the president if you work in government, your parents if you are a child, your teacher if you are a student, your coach if you are an athlete, your commanding officer if you are in the military, and so on.

The Individual Responsibility Principle

All of us are individually responsible for our own destiny. If you succeed, it's because you deserve it; if you fail, it's your own fault. You're on your own, and you should be. No coddling.

The Free-Market Principle

The free market promotes efficiency, creates wealth, is natural and moral, and rewards individual discipline. Since wealth can provide many freedoms, the free market is a mechanism of freedom and there should be no interference from government. It interferes in the free market in four ways: regulation, workers' rights (worker safety, pensions, overtime pay, etc.), taxation (takes away the rewards of the market), and class-action lawsuits that cost money. People's needs—save physical security—should be met through the market.

The Bootstraps Principle

With enough self-discipline, *everyone* can pull himself or herself up by the bootstraps. The government has no responsibility to help people who have fallen behind, because it's their own fault, caused by lack of discipline and morality. Charity is an act of individual virtue, not a responsibility of government.

CAUSATION THEORIES:
POVERTY AND TERRORISM

In surveying conservative and progressive arguments, we have noticed another important regularity. Conservatives seem to argue on the basis of direct, individual causation, while progressives tend to argue on the basis of systemic, complex causation. Two prime examples are terrorism and poverty.

Conservatives see terrorism in simple terms: evil people whose conduct is inexcusable and therefore unworthy of analysis. The most that conservatives will concede is that terrorists "hate our freedoms."[7]

Liberals tend to ask questions about the deeper, systemic causes of terrorism. Though liberals agree that the conduct is inexcusable, they consider what factors cause hatred of the United States: our military presence in Islamic countries, the absence of schools other than religious madrassas in those countries, our support of authoritarian monarchies in many Arab nations, and our active support of Israel.

This different understanding of the cause of terrorism translates into different solutions. Conservatives respond with little more than meeting force with force. Liberals consider whether long-term solutions require something other than military action, such as engaging the "battle of ideas" in the Middle East. In such a battle, all sorts of options are on the table, ranging from pushing allies like Saudi Arabia to democratize their nations and working more aggressively to solve the Israeli/Palestinian conflict.

Regarding the causes of poverty, conservatives lay the blame squarely on the poor. The American dream is available to anyone who is disciplined, moral, and enterprising. The poor are by definition lazy and immoral—simply not willing to lift themselves by their bootstraps.

Liberals see a more complex set of factors: Educational disadvantages, cultural biases, the vestiges of racism, entrenched institutions, as well as some government policies are all seen as contributing to entrenched poverty. Liberals deride the growing gap between rich and poor, while conservatives see it as a natural consequence of a just free market.

The same direct vs. systemic causation dichotomy occurs in a host of areas, such as crime, health care, environment, international relations, immigration, and more.

These different outlooks are predictable and flow from the different family models. In the strict father model, children get direct commands and are punished directly if they don't obey. Their transgressions are individual and so is their punishment. This is consistent with fundamentalist religion, where individual sins—or lack of them—determine whether one is headed for heaven or hell. In the nurturant parent model, children develop morally via attachment and empathy, which require an attunement to complex situations and contextual factors.

This presents liberals with a challenge, because in our sound-bite culture, it can be difficult to persuade with complex arguments. The answer is not to cede to a simplistic but ineffective solution to complex problems. In Chapter 8, we offer some suggestions for dealing with these complicated issues with consistent, authentic, values-based communications.

IDENTITY ISSUES: GAYS AND ABORTION

Why should someone in a long-term, stable, and loving heterosexual marriage be threatened if a gay or lesbian couple in a similar relationship were to marry?

Imagine that you are a pure conservative and your worldview is shaped by the strict father model applied to every aspect of your life. It defines your very *identity*: your notion of right and wrong, of God, of what makes a good parent, and of how to run a successful business. It even defines your maleness or femaleness, your sexual identity.

The strict father model is gendered. It has a male husband and a female wife. The parents in that model cannot be lesbian or gay. Legitimizing gay marriage *delegitimizes* the strict father model. The "defense of marriage" is really a defense of the strict father model. Being against "gay marriage" is symbolic of defending an identity defined by the strict father model—defending who you are at the very core of your being.

The abortion issue works in a similar way. In the idealized strict father model, the father is the moral authority; he controls reproduction decisions. He decides whether to use birth control, whether to have children, and whether his wife can have an abortion. He is responsible for his daughter's sexuality, and he will decide whether she should have sex education, whether she should have sex, and whether she can use birth control. And if she gets pregnant out of wedlock, he decides whether she should have an abortion.

Even the notion of abortion as murder comes from the strict father model, where there is an absolute right and an absolute wrong. That means all categories that appear in moral law must have strict defining conditions, especially the category of a human being. In philosophy, those defining conditions are called "essences," and they cannot change over time. So the essence of being human, which is there right at birth, must have also been there right before birth, and the day before that and the day before that, back to the moment of conception! Abortion must therefore be the purposeful killing of a human being for one's own benefit—murder!

CONSERVATIVE POPULISM

Liberals have generally failed to understand the nature of conservative populism. They tend to be puzzled that poor and middle-class conservatives vote against their own economic interests. The stereotype is that conservative populists are not too bright, are uninformed, and are being bamboozled by rich conservatives. The cure, liberals think, is telling them the truth. Just get the right information and get them to understand the economic facts of the matter, and they will all become economic populists and vote with progressives. It's a pipe dream.

Conservative populism is *cultural* in nature. That's what the conservatives' "culture war" is about. Conservative populists have a strict father morality and an identity based on it. Accordingly, they tend to reason about politics with direct causation, not systemic causation. But most important, they have been convinced by the conservative message machine that they are being oppressed—by the literal elite! They think they're being sneered at by the limousine liberals, the Hollywood liberals, the sushi-eating, latte-sipping liberals. They believe they're being lied to by the liberal media, that their money is being stolen by tax-and-spend liberals, that their private property is being endangered by liberal environmentalists, that their businesses are being squeezed by the liberal unions, that their religion is under attack by the godless liberals, and that their family is under threat from liberal feminists and gays. The word they use most to characterize their political aspirations is "liberty," which means freedom from the oppression of a political and cultural elite.[8]

Rational appeals to their economic well-being won't change them.

Here is the only hope we see: Reach out to those who are biconceptual and identify with their partial progressive values—values they genuinely share with progressives. On the basis of that identity, convince them of an important truth, that they are being oppressed by conservatives—the land they love is being destroyed by conservatives, their progressive Christianity is under severe attack by conservative fundamentalists, their very bodies and their families' bodies are under attack by conservatives. There is no lack of arguments to make here.

Without an understanding of the role of strict father morality in American culture, there is no hope of activating progressive aspects of their being.

5

MORALITY AND THE MARKET

You hear it all the time from conservatives: "Leave it to the market." Health care: Leave it to the market. Social Security: Leave it to the market. The climate crisis: Leave it to the market. Campaign finance: Leave it to the market. Minimum wage: Leave it to the market.

The market even plays a major role in our foreign policy. The Iraq war was partly about bringing markets to Iraqis. Much of our government's efforts in international relations are about fostering "free markets" through "free-trade policies." Privatization and deregulation convey the same message: Leave it to the market. America is a market economy. Progressives function just fine in America's markets, and a great many do very well in the marketplace and celebrate it. Yet progressives—even the wealthy ones—tend to disagree with virtually all of the leave-it-to-the-market arguments.

What's going on? Do conservatives and liberals mean different things by "the market," and, if so, what are they? And why are conservatives seen as the only—or at least the primary—champions of the market?

Interestingly, we've discovered that the family models discussed in the last chapter structure our understanding not only of government and national politics but of a host of other social institutions—global politics, schools, the church, and sports teams, for example. The market is among them.

There is a widely hailed conservative version of the market and a largely implicit, intuitively understood—but rarely articulated—progressive version. It is crucial to understand the difference.

Markets are institutions for the exchange of "goods and services," which can be almost anything, including money or stocks. Other products include convenience, identity (intimately connected with branding), and risk insurance. Even one's labor is conceptualized as a product that one—or one's union—sells in a labor market.

The classical assumption behind markets is that everyone is trying to maximize profit, with sellers trying to maximize prices and buyers trying to minimize costs. This leads to the idea of the market as "determining value"—what the buyer is willing to pay and the seller is willing to accept.

The central idea, promulgated by Adam Smith, is that everyone is, or should be, trying to maximize his or her profit. By what Smith termed the "invisible hand," that is, as a matter of nature, such a market maximizes profit for the totality of buyers and sellers and so helps everyone—including the nation.[1]

This is the idealization. It is seen as moral because it is seen as natural for everyone to maximize his or her own profit—the system Smith described is an accurate account of how the world, or at least the economic world, works.

The idealization makes many assumptions that economists know are not really true: There is near-perfect competition, there is perfect knowledge by both buyers and sellers, there is equal accessibility, there is no collusion by sellers to inflate prices, both buyer and seller are equally powerful, and both buyers and sellers act rationally.

These assumptions are false, and the fact that they are false raises serious questions about the natural and moral aspects of markets of many kinds. Nonetheless, it is widely assumed—by both liberals and conservatives—that the idealization is true.

These are factual assumptions about how the economic world works. But when the question turns to values—how *should* the market function?—the answers informed by the strict and nurturant family models differ markedly. And problems with the idealization become more noticeable.

CONSERVATIVE IDOLATRY

In the strict father model, the "free market" plays a significant, implicit role. The market is a competitive system where the disciplined are rewarded through profit, and the undisciplined (and hence immoral) are punished through poverty. The market is an instrument of morality. Because the "free market" is seen as being natural, moral, and fair, the following strict father logic applies: If you're not prosperous, it means you're not disciplined; if you're not disciplined, you cannot be moral, and therefore you deserve your poverty.

The market is to fundamentalist economics what God is to fundamentalist religion—God rewards the disciplined people who follow His commandments and punishes sinners who are undisciplined or rebellious. As with fundamentalist religion, the conservative's market is radically individualist. You and you alone are responsible for whether you go to heaven or hell and whether you succeed or fail in the market. Like God, the market rewards or punishes, depending on how disciplined you are.

There are a number of entailments that come along with this conservative view of the economy.

The profit motive is taken as ensuring maximum efficiency, so the market satisfies individual needs best. Government is seen as wasteful and inefficient, interfering with the idealized "free" market. It interferes in four ways:

- *Regulation*, which limits what individuals or corporations can do to make profits
- *Taxes*, which are seen as taking profits away
- *Workers' rights and unions*, which lessen corporate and investor profits
- *Tort lawsuits*, which can take away corporate and investor profits

That is why the right wing is for deregulation, against taxation, against unions and workers' rights, and for "tort reform."

Also, in conservative economics (as with conservative religion), the Earth is to be used by human beings for their profit. Nature is there for the benefit of man. Things that aren't privatized and being used for production have no value. Therefore, as much as can be privatized should be turned over for development. There is no room for the idea of a commons—a common inheritance of all mankind in the natural world—that should be protected from being commoditized and used for individual profit.

PROGRESSIVE MORALITY

For progressives—who start with empathy for others and responsibility for both themselves and others—markets should serve to make people free: free from want, free from harm, free from fear, free to meet one's needs and fulfill one's dreams. In short, the job of markets is to serve the common good; allow everyone who works to earn a decent living; help achieve freedom from want, illness, harm, ignorance, bigotry, and fear; preserve the natural world; and serve democracy.

Progressives are focused on where markets depart from the idealization, where markets fail to meet expectations, and where government is necessary. With these goals that define market success, progressives are acutely aware of what they see as real or potential market "failures" or "excesses" that require a government role to allow markets to function and serve the common good.

All the things that radical conservatives see as harmful government interference in free markets, progressives see as absolutely necessary government support for the *success* of markets:

- *Regulation* protects the public from harmful products and fraud by unscrupulous or irresponsible businesses.
- *Taxation* brings together the common wealth to build a common infrastructure that we all need to fulfill our individual needs and dreams. Progressive taxation is fair: Those who benefit most from the common wealth should pay the most to sustain it.
- *Unions and workers' rights* help balance the unfair distribution of power in job negotiations and promote safe, healthy, and ethical workplaces.
- *Tort lawsuits* are the last possibility—the baseline of protection—for dissuading irresponsible companies from harming the public.

As mentioned above, the common good principle is central here: The common wealth has been used to build highways, develop the Internet and the satellite system, uphold the banking system, regulate the stock market, and support the court system, which guarantees contracts. No business functioning in the market could exist without massive use of the common wealth. It is crucial to the existence and flourishing of markets. And those who benefit from markets have a moral obligation to replenish the common wealth.

Progressives see markets as serving a moral purpose—a progressive moral purpose. And they recognize a truth that conservative ideology hides: Markets can't thrive and serve the common good without the constructive role of government. This is what conservatives ignore when they speak of the "free market."

THE FREE-MARKET MYTHOLOGY

The conservative idealization of the "free market" falls far short of reality. Indeed, expectations of living up to this ideal are quite harmful. Here's what is in the conservative's free-market frame:

> Markets are free when government doesn't regulate or interfere in the market. Through the "invisible hand," markets maximize efficiency and wealth for all. Government "intervention" in the market stifles freedom, creates inefficiency and waste, and inhibits profitability for all. Free markets are open and accessible to all. Seeking profit in the market is natural, moral, and fair. Because markets maximize profit overall, they contribute to freedom. Ensuring free markets is thus a moral cause.

Nice as this may sound, the "free market" is a myth, *and conservatives well know it!* They understand that government regulation of and participation in the market can be beneficial. For instance, the staunchest free-market proponents in Congress and the administration didn't bat an eye after 9/11 when they bailed out the airlines to the tune of $15 billion on the basis that the airline industry is a vital part of the nation.[2] They send a large percentage of the federal budget year after year to private defense companies, shifting public wealth to private owners. They spend tens of billions to support the oil industry.[3] They maintain price supports for agribusiness to keep profits high and the price of food low.[4] For generations, they have auctioned off or given public resources like the airwaves and land, water, and oil rights to corporations for development.

These are cases of the *upward redistribution of wealth*—transfers of wealth from ordinary taxpayers to wealthy owners, managers, and stockholders. These interventions in the market promote what conservatives believe is the vital national interest.

But when government intervenes on behalf of working people, consumers, or the environment, conservatives scream foul and invoke the "free-market" frame, because these interventions don't mesh with their political philosophy. "Free market" is a slogan used to attack the essential rules that keep the market functioning for the common good. It's time to end the "free-market" myths.

Myth 1: A Purely "Free Market" Is Ideal. Consider what a purely free market—that is, a market without government intervention—would look like. Drug companies could market drugs they haven't fully tested, knowing they cannot be regulated or sued. A mining company's only incentive to secure safety for its workers would be the fear that killing too many workers would decrease the labor supply and drive up labor costs or generate ill will. An oil company's only incentive to strip gasoline of lead would be the potential PR problem from putting lead in our atmosphere. Indeed, the early days of the Industrial Revolution mirrored this world, and it was a very difficult time for workers. A "free market" means business can strip the commons of its wealth, making the rest of us pay for its profits.

Myth 2: People Are Rational Actors. A central assumption behind the free market is that consumers are "rational" and always act to maximize their self-interest. We now know from cognitive science and psychology research that people do not really think that way. Frames, metaphors, prototypes, and other nonlogical cognitive mechanisms enter crucially into their decisions. Consumers don't make decisions based on perfect cost-benefit

analyses; they also base them on simplifying assumptions, an un-
equal weighting of risk and reward, different attitudes about
"found" money and earned money, and other factors. This puts
consumers at a disadvantage in the market when dealing with
maximally efficient corporations.

Myth 3: There Is a Level Playing Field. Companies have
two kinds of employees—assets (upper management and creative
people) and resources (people who are interchangeable and
available in the "labor market"). Profits rise when the cost of resources falls; the pressure to increase profits correspondingly
tends to drive down wages. From a market perspective, a job
seeker wants to sell his or her labor, and the company wants to
buy that labor for as little as possible. Unemployment helps prof-
itability by producing competition among job seekers, which
tends to drive down "prices"—that is, wages. In such a situation,
individuals seeking work have very little, if any, leverage to increase their wages. The power belongs to the employer. Unions
help to balance that power by cornering the market on labor and
thus driving up the price that can be charged for it. The minimum wage sets a floor on how low employers can go in setting
prices for labor. In the *ideal* "free" market, which doesn't exist,
there is no such power differential. Conservatives who oppose
unions and the minimum wage argue that in such a "free market," wages should be set by the market, and anything else is unfair. In real markets, the playing field between employees and
employers is anything but level.

Myth 4: A Company's Balance Sheet Reflects True Costs.
It is commonplace for businesses to externalize costs and have
the government or the public pay for them. Many companies do
not pay to dispose of their waste but instead just pollute the air
or water, passing on to the public the costs of doing business.
Many businesses extract resources—oil, minerals, timber—on
government-owned land for a fraction of what they would pay
on the open market. These are publicly owned resources, and the

"true cost" is being borne by the public. Other businesses make the public work for them for free. When you make a "customer service" call and then have to wait interminably, *your* time is being used so that the company doesn't have to hire more people to handle customer service calls. *You* are working for the company. The same is true when a company tells customers to look up information on its Web site. It is the customer's time and effort being spent. These are ways to "externalize" true costs and make more profit. Progressives who want to ban the externalization of costs are ultimately working to make markets closer to ideal "free markets."

Myth 5: Everything, Even Life, Has a Fair Monetary Value. How can a market assign adequate value to a human life? An endangered species? A healthy ecosystem? Aesthetics? In a purely free market, value is determined through supply and demand, with calculation done via cost-benefit analysis. Life insurance companies assign a dollar value to human life. Corporations use cost-benefit analysis to decide how safe to make a car or a drug. HMOs use cost-benefit analysis to determine whether it is "worth it" to send a patient to a specialist, or to have an MRI taken. The "free-market" frame assumes that these are "fair costs" and that the process is always moral. The fact is that there is no such thing as a "fair price" for these things.

Myth 6: Markets Are Outside the Scope of Moral Judgments. The conservative view is that unconstrained free markets are *inherently* natural and fair—and inherently moral, in that they maximize profits for everyone. But, as we have seen, business decisions affect human health and life, the survival of species, and so on. These are moral factors, and we cannot afford to ignore them.

Myth 7: Everyone Can Pull Himself or Herself Up by the Bootstraps. While it is true that any individual may, in fact, be able to pull himself or herself up by the bootstraps, it is *not* true that *all* people can do so. Our economy is structured by a cheap labor trap—it depends on the people who flip burgers, wait tables, garden, clean up slaughterhouses, and pick fruits and vegetables. A lot of these workers cannot pull themselves up, because the jobs aren't there for everyone; neither is the start-up capital to employ all of them. And if they did manage to pull themselves up, who would do that work?

GOVERNMENT VS. MARKET

The "free-market frame" is not an innocent description. It has major moral implications: Privatization and deregulation are seen as virtues that lead to "less government." That is a fallacy. They lead to less *responsible* government.

Let's look at a new idea: the conservation of governance. In general, governance is about making decisions. In some spheres, governance is best solved through personal autonomy, allowing individuals to make choices to determine the course of their own lives—where they want to live, what they will read, what clothes they will wear, what food to eat—so long as these choices do not impinge on the ability of others to make those same choices. In other spheres, governance is best left to the market, to determine what prices we pay for typical consumer goods. Communist and socialist societies have shown that planned economies do not work very well. In the public sphere, decisions should be made through democratic institutions—who our elected leaders will be, where and how the government will spend its money, what our environment will look like, and what are acceptable standards for those participating in the market.

But a dangerous shift in decision-making power is taking place. This is being driven by the conservative emphasis on privatization and deregulation. HMOs and drug companies, for instance, are deciding what type of medical care people will have and how much it will cost. (The recent prescription drug bill *prevents* Medicare from even negotiating volume discounts with drug companies.) Car companies are deciding how much CO_2 we can put in our atmosphere and how fuel-efficient our cars will be. The energy industry determines what type of energy we have access to, its impact on the environment, and how much it will cost. Private testing companies determine what kids should learn and how they should learn it.

These are moral decisions that affect the common good. As such, they should be publicly discussed, and the decision makers should be known and accountable to the public. In short, they should be made by democratically elected government, not corporate government, so they are ideally made in the interest of the public (though government can be manipulated to benefit special interests). But when government functions are privatized and industries are deregulated, these decisions are made in boardrooms for the benefit of stockholder profits. Because corporations are legally bound to maximize profit for their stockholders, and since spending on public safety and other aspects of the public good takes away from profits, corporate governments have an incentive *not* to work for the common good.

Privatization and deregulation constitute *the outsourcing of democratically elected government with a moral mission* to corporations that have a profit-making mission. The effect is to turn *democracy* into *corporatocracy*.

PROFIT AND HUMAN DIGNITY

Unfortunately, the conservative view of the unregulated "free market" has captured the imagination of many Americans, because conservatives have effectively communicated this idea for some time. Terms like the "free market" or assumptions like "you can spend your money better than the government can" establish the debate on conservative terms, making it difficult, if not impossible, for progressives to put forward their ideals.

What alternative frame can we use? How do we center the debate on questions that are important to us and not to conservatives?

On issue after issue, the counterpoints to the conservative principle of the free market are the progressive principles of *human dignity* and the *common good*. We are interested in a market that serves human values, not humans who serve a market.

Take the issue of health care. Conservatives believe that people should get as much or as little health care as the market provides based on your wealth. For conservatives, health care is essentially a commodity, like cotton or coal. Progressives believe that there is some basic acceptable standard of health care that must be available to all, by virtue of being an American and a human being. This is what it means to take human dignity seriously. A person's health should not be left to the vagaries of the marketplace, particularly given the great wealth of this nation. Progressives also believe that healthy citizens will mean a healthy nation as a whole. Disease, after all, is transmittable. Failure to cure some of us can lead to the spread of disease to a great many of us.

In the conservatives' worldview, even the environment is subject to market demands. They believe that the market should determine how much clean air and clean water is worth and that this determination should be subject to a cost-benefit analysis. A clean environment is simply another commodity. That overrides any responsibility as a community to preserve it for our children. Progressives believe that there is an inalienable right to clean air and clean water and that every human being deserves it—again as a matter of human dignity and the common good.

When it comes to education, conservatives believe that the market should decide how much of an education you get. No free rides. They apply the issues of "competition" and "consumer choice" to schooling. Progressives believe that human dignity and the successful functioning of a democracy require that all Americans receive a decent education.

The same goes for welfare, for Social Security, for transportation, and so on. Again and again, the conservative free market says that there is no floor, that it's inevitable that many people will be losers. This contrasts sharply with the progressive view that markets must respect human dignity and serve the common good while pursuing profit. Each person's dreams depend on the common good.

MARKET FAILURES

Thirty years ago, the richest 1 percent owned less than a fifth of America's wealth. Now, according to a recent report by the Federal Reserve Board, they own over a third.[5] Is there anything wrong with that picture? Conservatives tend to say no—it is a natural consequence of the free market, which is fair. If you, or your ancestors, have accumulated $1 billion or $10 billion in the free market, that is fair.

But that assumes you have earned your money on your own, or that some of your ancestors have. But we know from the principle of the common wealth for the common good that no one makes it on his or her own in this country, and that the more you make, the more you have used the common wealth, and the more responsibility you have to pay to maintain the common wealth.

Another way to look at it is that not all of it is "your" money—money you earned all by yourself with no dependence on anyone. Great wealth can be accumulated only by using other people's money—through infrastructure paid for by taxpayers and through transfers of wealth directly from taxpayers to you, through government subsidies, writing off business expenses, tax breaks, no-bid contracts, and so on. These are transfers of wealth from ordinary citizens to the wealthy, and should be discussed as such. The common wealth infrastructure is one of the glories of American capitalism. It is there to be used by all, but if you make great wealth, you have a responsibility to pay back an appropriate amount to maintain that common wealth infrastructure so others can use it, too. The estate tax is the easiest way to pay back. You don't have to pay it till you're dead. And your heirs, who didn't earn it, still get half of that great wealth.

Some months ago Rockridge received a note from a thirty-year-old man in Hawaii, who grew up there and had always lived there. He can no longer afford to. So many wealthy people have bought second and third homes there that many ordinary working people can no longer afford to buy a home in that market, or in his case, even pay the rent on an apartment. In short, the wealthy are investing their money in scarce resources like second, third, and fourth homes in beautiful places. This tends to limit access to the nicer but scarce things in life to the ultrarich. When the tsunami wiped out beautiful fishing villages in South Asia, they were all too often replaced by resort hotels on the beach and mansions for the rich—and the traditional fishermen were left without their ancestral homes. The pre–Hurricane Katrina ordinary residents of the nicest parts of the Louisiana coast may be in for this fate as well. Again, these are transfers of wealth to the wealthy. The issue is more than the money itself—the issue is access to the wonderful but scarce wonders of everyday life, starting with real estate.

We began with the false idealization of "free markets" by conservatives who believe that near-perfect competition exists, that buyers and sellers are equal players, that there is free choice, and so on.

But deviations are everywhere. Corporate consolidation—

"mergers and acquisitions"—in industry after industry has greatly limited competition and pushed up prices and profits by transferring more wealth from ordinary people to the wealthy. Deregulation has given corporations a great knowledge advantage over consumers; corporations, not consumers, know which drugs are harmful, or which cars will break down, or when the paint will peel off. Large corporations have much more market access—say, to supermarket shelves—than small businesses. Collusion on pricing is widespread and has become sophisticated. You don't have a free choice about buying lifesaving prescription drugs. Wal-Mart is far more powerful than the people it hires in its nonunion shop. And every marketer knows that consumers do not act rationally. The "free market" isn't free.

Markets have moral functions, and they are constructed to meet moral values and principles. Conservatives have been defining markets to fit their moral worldview. Progressives are way behind. It's time to speak out.

6

FUNDAMENTAL VALUES

These two models of the conservative and progressive world-views show a drastically divergent set of principles. And yet over and over, we find that both conservative and progressive politicians talk about the same set of values—fairness, equality, responsibility, freedom, integrity, and security. Often, there is agreement about what they are saying. For all our political differences, we share far more ideals in common as Americans than one would think from all the harsh rhetoric of Sunday morning talk shows.

In some cases, though, conservatives and progressives have very different ideas about what a value means.

For example, Congressman John Murtha of Pennsylvania was seen by progressives as *courageous* for coming out in late 2005 against continuing the American occupation of Iraq. They saw him as supporting American troops in an impossible situation. They believed the occupation should end. But conservatives saw Murtha as a *coward* for taking what they labeled a "cut and run" position, which they saw as failing to support our troops. One person's paragon of courage became another person's coward.

Another example is what we might call the "freedom to marry" movement, which sees same-sex marriage as an issue of personal freedom. The government should not be involved in perhaps the most important moral and personal decision in your life: whom you marry. Progressives liken the situation to the expansion of freedom when the old laws banning interracial marriage were overturned.

George W. Bush also considers this a "freedom" issue, but he argued it to the opposite conclusion on June 5, 2006, when Congress took up a constitutional amendment to ban "gay marriage":

> In our free society, decisions about a fundamental social institution as marriage should be made by the people. The American people have spoken clearly on this issue through their elected representatives and at the ballot box. In 1996, Congress approved the Defense of Marriage Act by large bipartisan majorities in both the House and the Senate, and President Clinton signed it into law. And since then, 19 states have held referendums to amend their state constitutions to protect the traditional definition of marriage. In every case, the amendments were approved by decisive majorities with an average of 71 percent.[1]

In the progressive worldview, this is a matter of personal freedom beyond government rule. In the conservative worldview, the government has the moral authority to decide, and freedom is the exercise of the vote by elected officials.

What produces such cases is the fact that the concepts expressed by words such as "freedom" are *contested*. A contested concept is an idea that means different things to different people. The British political scientist W. B. Gallie, using examples like "art" and "democracy," first described their properties in the late 1950's.[2] Gallie and others, especially linguists, have noticed certain regularities about contested concepts:

- Each such concept has an uncontested core that is generally agreed on—an example or class of examples that there is no argument about.

- Each such concept is evaluative, that is, expresses certain values, and the contestation arises from value differences.
- Each such uncontested version of the concept has a complex structure, and contested versions are variations on that structure.

It used to be believed among philosophers and political scientists that if a concept was contested, it could have no clear logic. The situation was just a mess with different people having arbitrarily different views. But since people repeatedly use contested concepts in arguments in an understandable way, that itself suggests there is a logic where conclusions can be drawn. And indeed there is. The system was discovered by cognitive scientists Alan Schwartz and George Lakoff.[3]

Let's take a look at six crucial American values—and how the progressive and conservative understandings of them differ, as well as how these differences are structured by the family models and political principles discussed in Chapter 4.

FAIRNESS

The following voting principle links fairness and equality: It is fair for everyone's vote to count equally. Nobody's vote counts twice as much as another's, and no person's vote is not counted.

This is a core principle that everyone agrees with—as long as we disregard the hard cases: Should absentee military votes in Florida have been counted in 2004 if they were sent in after the election ended, when it was known that the election was close? Should confusing butterfly ballots have been recast? Does a hanging chad count? The contested concept was that of a *vote*.

The logical statement of voting fairness is possible if we rule out the contested meaning of *vote*. Applying this more generally, we can state the uncontested core of the fairness concept: *Fairness is unbiased distribution*.

Most conservatives and progressives would agree on that principle. The idea of fairness contains other concepts, though, that are contested: *bias, a process of distributing things, things distributed, who they are distributed to*, and so on. What counts as "bias"? What is to count as an appropriate process for distributing things? What counts as an appropriate thing to be distributed?

Applying either the strict father (conservative) or nurturant parent (progressive) model to these questions typically yields different answers. It is these models that structure the contested category of *fairness*.

To see how this works, consider the issue of affirmative action in admissions to public colleges and universities.

To progressives, affirmative action is motivated by empathy and is fair and right.

First is empathy for African Americans and Native Americans, who often live in communities that are still suffering from past discrimination.

Second is empathy for poor minorities, who are often discriminated against culturally—given inferior educations or the lack of cultural knowledge necessary to succeed in the business world.

Third is empathy for minority communities that commonly lack adequate professionals (doctors, nurses, dentists, and lawyers), social services, and a business infrastructure (banks, stock brokers, real estate agents, and corporation offices).

Affirmative action is designed to meet the moral mission of colleges and universities by making sure that all people, regardless of race or ethnicity, can realize the benefit of higher education. Universities are part of the common wealth—even private universities, which get much of their money from government grants and tax breaks from their nonprofit status—and should serve the common good. That means they should serve all sectors of society.

With affirmative action, colleges and universities can train students from a wide range of backgrounds, so they can return to their communities as doctors, lawyers, teachers, social service providers, and business owners and executives. This would raise the economic and educational levels, thereby helping to improve those communities over time. Affirmative action is about fairness, for redressing widespread *unfairness*.

Conservatives view fairness through the lens of the bootstraps principle. If you haven't made it, it's your own fault. If people work hard, they can make it. Everyone is subject to the same process, so everything is fair. To conservatives, affirmative action is simply unfair and immoral—a matter of giving people something (college admission) that they haven't earned.

Conservatives see college admissions in a different frame than progressives: a competition among individuals for a reward, namely, admission to a university that will allow one to make more money in the future. As a competition, it is a process that should be fair and unbiased. It should be about individual initiative and individual discipline. To be unbiased, colleges should use only "objective" criteria—grades on tests and in classes.

From such a perspective, progressive empathy is irrelevant. The needs of communities are irrelevant. Cultural discrimination is irrelevant. Past discrimination is irrelevant. The only things relevant are individual discipline, initiative, and achievement as shown by test scores.

This difference was highlighted in 1996 with Proposition 209—the "California Civil Rights Initiative."[4] Here is the main provision:

The state shall not discriminate against, or grant preferential treatment to, any individual or group on the basis of race, sex, color, ethnicity, or national origin in the operation of public employment, public education, or public contracting.

It sounds like it ends discrimination, and many progressives voted for it because they accepted the conservative frame for college admissions: a competition among individuals for a reward. Seen that way, affirmative action looks like discrimination.

But Prop 209 ended programs that were designed to remedy past discrimination. It sanctioned ongoing *systemic* discrimination. In short, Prop 209 was possible because fairness is a contested concept, and conservatives exploited its contested nature, while progressives fell into the conservative framing trap.

FREEDOM

We Americans have insisted throughout our history that certain freedoms be expanded: voting rights, civil rights, and the freedoms afforded by expanded systems of public education, public health, highways, parks, libraries, and scientific research. These are progressive freedoms.

But they are being turned back in the name of a very different concept of freedom—a radical conservative "freedom" that fits modern conservative ideology. Conservatives have taken over the words "freedom," "free," and "liberty." Bush, in his second inaugural address in January 2005, used those words forty-nine times in twenty minutes.[5] Turn to the Web sites of Jerry Falwell[6] and James Dobson,[7] and it's liberty this and liberty that—Liberty University, Liberty Counsel, Liberty Alerts.

This is because freedom is also a classic case of an essentially contested concept.

Uncontested freedom is (very roughly) defined as *being able to do what you want to do, providing you don't interfere with the freedom of others*. This includes physical freedom, freedom to pursue goals, freedom of the will, and political freedom, where citizens freely choose who runs the state and where the state, by law, cannot interfere with the basic freedoms of its citizens. This much is generally accepted.

In addition, there is a logic of what counts as interfering with one's freedom, a logic that includes such notions as *coercion, harm, property, opportunity, fairness, justice, rights, responsibility, nature,* and *competition*. Here is a sketch of that logic:

- *Coercion* and *harm*, and the fear of them, interfere with one's freedom.
- *Property* and *money* add to one's freedom. Conversely, the taking of your property or money is an imposition on your freedom.
- *Opportunity* is necessary for freedom.
- *Unfairness* interferes with freedom by taking from you what is rightfully yours.
- *Justice* contributes to freedom, since it deters unfairness, coercion, and harm.
- *Rights* give you access; to take away access is to interfere with freedom.
- *Responsibility* must be exercised, usually by others, to make your rights possible. Freedom of access thus requires that others exercise *responsibility*.
- *Nature* cannot interfere with freedom; only people can. If your legs are broken in an earthquake, the earthquake has not interfered with your freedom. But if they are broken by a Mafia enforcer, then he has interfered with your freedom.

- *Competition* does not involve freedom: The winner in a competition is not interfering with the freedom of the loser.

That is the basic logic of *uncontested* freedom—as long as you stick to the uncontested meanings of coercion, harm, property, nature, competition, and so on. Freedom becomes contested when these concepts become contested.

To get a sense of the contestation, consider what constitutes "interference" with freedom. Do I have a right to say what I want, even if it's obscene, or do you have a right not to be offended (interfered with)? Do we have a *responsibility* to extend freedoms to others to give them *opportunities*? If I have no clothes, no food, and no shelter, am I free? How much *property* is necessary for adequate freedom? Should we collect taxes from those with the most to enhance the freedoms of those with much less? As you can see, the uncontested notion of freedom can get quite complicated very quickly.

These questions indicate that freedom is highly contested. But, as with fairness, there is a logic to the answers. They are filled in by the parent models discussed in Chapter 4. Typically, application of one model or the other to these questions will yield different answers, so you get two very different forms of freedom.

Apply "strict father" morality to the components of uncontested freedom, and you get conservative freedom; apply the "nurturant" morality, and you get progressive freedom.

For instance, progressives and conservatives both recognize that *property* can enhance one's freedom. Progressives, based on the "human dignity principle," recognize freedom from want as a fundamental freedom: Acting on *empathy* for people who are down and out requires that we have a social safety net to secure their freedom. So progressives see Social Security, welfare, and universal health care as increasing freedom.

Conservatives take the opposite approach. They start from the idea that *self-discipline* is fundamental. A lack of property to conservatives indicates a lack of discipline, and hence a lack of morality. Therefore, giving people things they haven't earned creates dependency, which traps people in welfare programs and poverty and thus robs them of their freedom. Not only that, but the taxes that pay for programs like Social Security and universal health care infringe on the freedom of the taxpayer, since taking his money is imposing on his freedom.

What progressives see as essential freedoms, conservatives see as essential interferences.

Consider different approaches to the market.

The Progressive Argument

Progressives empathize with people suffering economic hardship in the world's richest nation and believe that economic pressures can deny people their freedoms. For instance, if you have to work eighty hours a week at the minimum wage of $5.15 to earn poverty wages, the market is interfering with your freedom—freedom from want, freedom of opportunity. So progressives see regulation of the market as an issue of freedom. In accordance with the "common good principle," progressives also believe that Social Security, universal health care, and access to a college education—all part of the common wealth—can help the impoverished improve their finances, thereby contributing to freedom from want.

The Conservative Argument

Conservatives, on the other hand, believe that the market is a "natural" system. As a "natural" phenomenon, the market—like an earthquake or a rainstorm—can't interfere with people's freedom. The government should not set "artificial" prices for the market. A statute that says an employer and an employee can't engage in a contract for less than $5.15 an hour is interfering with the natural functioning of the market and thus inhibiting freedom. So regulations of the natural free market are interfering with freedom.

Conservatives' "strict" morality also dictates that discipline is what the market requires. It is the mechanism by which property is acquired. Property adds to one's freedom. A lack of discipline means a lack of property. A lack of property means a lack of freedom.

Lakoff's *Whose Freedom?* goes explicitly through the details of these and many more cases of how strict and nurturant morality yield opposite versions of freedom.

EQUALITY

In simple cases, equality is fairly straightforward. Two plus two equals three plus one. "Two plus two" and "three plus one" characterize the same amount. When you're dividing a pie equally among six kids, each kid gets a wedge of the same size. If a relatively small group of people is voting, equality means one person, one vote.

Therefore, in simple cases, equality has an uncontested core: *Equality is sameness of distribution.*

The *contested* issues are *what is distributed, who things are distributed to, what the process of distribution is, what counts as the same, who does the distributing,* and *on what basis.*

Things get even more complicated in social, legal, and political equality, where the *things distributed* are votes, rights, property, pollution credits, use of bandwidths, college admissions, jobs, access to legal counsel, marriage licenses, medical treatments, and so on. In religion, equality has to do with equal access to God versus access only through a priest or minister, the right to become a priest or minister, and so on. In politics, it is the question of which votes count, how they should be counted, who has the opportunity to run for office, who has access to office holders, and so on. Equality before the law means that everyone should be treated the same in the legal process, regardless of wealth or position.

To get a sense of how equality is contested in politics, consider the constant struggle between liberals and conservatives over what equality means: equality of opportunity versus equality of outcome.

Conservatives accept equality of opportunity—but it assumes the conservative deep frames, i.e., the market is open to everyone, so nothing further needs to be done except to get the government out of the way. It is all a matter of individual initiative and individual responsibility and individual accomplishment. Conservatives speak of "equity"—a hierarchy of merit, where merit is defined by success in the market. Equity replaces equality of outcome with a hierarchy of merit.

For progressives, empathy leads us to identify with the needs of others. A perfect example is President Lyndon B. Johnson's 1965 speech at the Howard University commencement:

> It is not enough to open the gates of opportunity; all our citizens must have the ability to walk through those gates. . . . We seek not just legal equity but human ability, not just equality as a right and a theory but equality as a fact and equality as a result. . . . To this end equal opportunity is essential, but not enough, not enough.[8]

Because progressives empathize with the other, we see the other as like us. Men and women of all races are born with the same range of abilities. Not the same abilities but the same range. Equality of outcome is therefore not identical outcomes but the same range of outcomes regardless of race. So we would expect that given *equality of opportunity* (as there should be in a democracy, and in a fair capitalist system), there would be equality of distribution of outcome. That is, if there were an equality of opportunity, there should be the same number of doctors, lawyers, scientists per capita in the African-American community as in the population at large. Or the median income in African-American households would be the same as in the population at large. But this is not the case. Given the assumption of the same range of abilities, this indicates that there must not be real equality of opportunity.

The "same range of abilities" frame is commonplace among liberals. It has a crucial use in classic liberal arguments. First, it defines the boundaries of racism: To deny it, to say some races have a greater range of abilities than others, is de facto taken as racist. Second, given this frame, it follows that different outcomes are de facto evidence of the effects of racism, past or present or both. The outcomes are documented in statistics—the rational presentation of a laundry list of statistical facts regarding infant mortality rates, income disparities, unemployment rates, and so on.

To counter the conservative argument that we should conclude from such facts that there is a racial difference of inborn abilities that have nothing to do with racism, LBJ, in his Howard University talk, spoke of the effects of racism on ability. Note that he took causes as not individual but as systemic and complex, both present and past:

> But ability is not just the product of birth. Ability is stretched or stunted by the family that you live with, and the neighborhood you live in—by the school you go to and the poverty or the richness of your surroundings. It is the product of a hundred unseen forces playing upon the little infant, the child, and finally the man.
>
> We know the causes are complex and subtle. . . .
>
> First, Negroes are trapped—as many whites are

trapped—in inherited, gate-less poverty. They lack training and skills. They are shut in, in slums, without decent
medical care. Private and public poverty combine to crip-
ple their capacities. . . .

We are trying to attack these evils through our poverty
program, through our education program, through our
medical care and our other health programs, and a dozen
more of the Great Society programs that are aimed at the
root causes of this poverty.

But there is a second cause—much more difficult to
explain, more deeply grounded, more desperate in its
force. It is the devastating heritage of long years of slavery; and a century of oppression, hatred, and injustice.

For Negro poverty is not white poverty. . . . These differences are not racial differences. They are solely and
simply the consequence of ancient brutality, past injustice, and present prejudice.

The reason we picked the LBJ speech was to show how much
the progressive issues, the frames, and the equality arguments
have remained the same over four decades, despite all the
changes.

One big move on the conservative side is toward having
equality replaced by equity—distribution on the basis of merit,
or *deservedness*. Conservatives and progressives differ in their understanding of *deservedness*, as one would predict, by the application of their respective moral systems.

For conservatives, *deservedness* is understood as the result
of discipline. Since their moral system advocates that reward
should be proportional to discipline and ability, *deservedness* reflects discipline and ability: hours worked, widgets manufactured,
or bold entrepreneurship, all of which hinge on being a disciplined person and so qualify as fair means for distributing resources *equitably*—by the market, not the government.

For progressives, *deservedness* is understood through the lens of *nurturance*, which says that someone *in need* deserves assistance. This satisfies the "human dignity principle," making sure no one falls too far behind. It also fulfills the "common good principle," since the needs of the commons are counted as valid needs that merit attention, besides just the needs of an individual.

The most recent conservative take on equality is via culture and family values. John McWhorter argues that the reason for a lack of African-American achievement is black culture, which does not respect learning, and so African-American kids grow up not doing well in school or in life.

David Brooks sees two cultural problems standing in the way of equality of outcome. The first is the breakdown in the nuclear family, which, he claims, has led to a lack of attachment between children and their parents. The second is that the culture does not support the delay of gratification. Both of these are conservative arguments that the government has no role to play in equality for African Americans. The cultural message is that the African-American community has to get its act together itself, learn to just say no, and start glorifying entrepreneurs, political leaders, and intellectuals over basketball players, hip-hop musicians, pimps, and criminals. The sneaky part of the McWhorter and Brooks argument is that they use nurturant values—responsibility and a respect for knowledge—as an argument *against* a progressive role for government.[9]

Interestingly, Brooks's recent discovery of attachment does not lead him to attack conservative child-rearing practices, e.g., James Dobson's Focus on the Family, which teaches strict father child rearing and its link to conservative politics.

RESPONSIBILITY

The difference in the conservative and progressive understanding of *responsibility* is conveniently reflected in a difference

between two surface frames English speakers have for understanding the word. This is instructive since the surface frame difference is one we can all understand and doesn't *necessarily* have
to do with one's moral system. Consider the following two ways
of talking about responsibility:

- Carrying the weight of a responsibility
- Fulfilling a responsibility

In the first, responsibility is a load carried by a single person as
she goes through life. This load makes moving through life more
difficult, and if the person is too weak to shoulder the responsibility, it is her fault and she alone is the failure. In the second,
there is a void that needs to be filled. If the person can't do it,
then she isn't the right person to fill the void, and someone else
more appropriate should be taking on the responsibility.

Progressive responsibility is connected with the surface frame
of fulfilling a need through empathy and using the common
wealth for the common good. An illustrative example of this is
Hurricane Katrina.

When disaster strikes, progressives generally react with empathy for those affected. In Katrina, it meant empathy for the victims of the hurricane and the ensuing breach of the levees. The
progressive vision has everyone helping in whatever capacity they
can. Our government has the powerful capability to harness our
collective resources. One way that we fulfill our responsibilities to
be nurturant of others is by paying taxes. Part of these taxes is to
be used by government to be the immediate responder in the aftermath of any disaster. When government does so, we can also
carry on with our personal responsibilities—working, taking care
of families, etc. The taxes we pay should have also been spent responsibly ensuring the safety of the levees in the first place.

The conservatives' response to Katrina was strikingly different. Instead of holding Bush and Secretary of Homeland Security Michael Chertoff responsible, they pushed blame downward

to the point where they blamed the victims themselves for choosing to live in and near New Orleans. Under the conservative principle of "individual responsibility," you are responsible for only yourself, so blaming the victims makes sense in their view. Bush can't be blamed if the government isn't supposed to be responsible for keeping the levees secure. For example, Joe Allbaugh, former FEMA director and Bush/Cheney campaign manager in 2000, argued before the Senate Appropriations Subcommittee that FEMA was an entitlement program to be phased out, not an agency essential to the safety of Americans. No responsibility was assumed.

Conservative responsibility also has two sides—the people making the rules and the people following the rules. It is the responsibility of our leaders to enforce discipline (moral authority), which means making rules and doling out rewards and punishment. For the rest of us, our responsibility is simply to follow the rules and otherwise maximize personal well-being—for ourselves and others.

The Katrina example has become such a major political touchstone because it highlights the two different attitudes about the role of government in our lives and about the contested concept of *responsibility*.

INTEGRITY

The basic logic of integrity is twofold. First, it means saying what you believe and then acting on it consistently. Second, it means the consistent application of a principle:

- Progressive integrity is the consistent application of nurturance.
- Conservative integrity is the consistent application of strictness.

It may seem simple, but these statements lead to an interesting difference in the understanding of integrity.

With discipline, constancy is critical. Discipline must be applied the same way every time, regardless of circumstance. The person being disciplined needs to understand that there is a direct and immediate consequence for all actions and that the consequence is the same. The focus is on the constancy of the process, the identicalness of action.

To consistently apply empathy, however, the needs of the person receiving nurturance must be addressed, not the process itself. So to remain empathetic, the same degree of care must be applied. Sometimes this care requires different actions or different approaches, depending on circumstance.

Moving back to politics, we can see this difference in the understanding of integrity in the conservative and progressive reaction to John Murtha's call to bring the troops back home. To progressives, Murtha was courageous and speaking out of empathy for the Iraqi people and, even more so, out of empathy for our troops. He knew he would receive withering criticism for doing so, but even still, he said what he believed. This unwavering dedication to nurturance and to his beliefs exemplifies the progressive view of integrity.

To conservatives, Murtha's initial commitment to the war and then his reversal were the exact opposite of courage and completely lacking in integrity. They see the Bush administration's unchanging vigilance in Iraq as a sign of integrity. What they fail to see in Murtha's case is that his initial support for the war was based on being misled to believe that it would protect Americans and protect Iraqis. In this respect, Murtha's commitment didn't change—his call for withdrawal reflected a continued interest in the safety of Americans, as did the initial decision to go to war based on flawed information.

So just as with fairness, equality, and freedom, integrity can be understood differently by conservatives and progressives because of a difference in worldview. The conservative worldview applies discipline to integrity to get an understanding of integrity that is unchanging action, regardless of changing circumstances. Progressive integrity comes from applying the idea of nurturance to integrity, the result being an unchanging commitment to nurturance, which may call for charting a different path when circumstance requires.

SECURITY

Progressives have been accused of being weak on security. However, this comes not from an objective assessment of progressive policies but rather from the fact that the conservative understanding of security has dominated public discourse. This is possible because *security* is a contested concept.

The uncontested core of security is *providing protection through strength.*

But strength itself is a contested concept, as can be seen in contrasting two different scenes. For the first scene, imagine a wall surrounding a city under attack. If the wall is strong, it will hold up against the attack, protecting the people inside. This is strength in the sense of protection against the use of force.

For the second scene, imagine a fist trying to punch through a board. If the person is strong, he or she will break through the board. This is strength through the use of force.

The first scene is representative of progressive security: security through protection. The second scene is representative of conservative security: security through the use of force.

The response of both ideologies to the threat of terrorism highlights this difference. The progressive response is to make sure our ports, our landmarks, our infrastructure, and our troops are protected. Progressives advocated for federal funds to be used to increase port security, for example, and wanted the Department of Homeland Security to protect possible targets of terrorist attack, not to turn itself into another pork-barrel slush fund.

The conservatives' strategy differed markedly. Their idea of security was to attack.

Some progressives voted for the use of force in both Afghanistan and Iraq because it was presumed that both wars would provide protection for Americans. When the Iraq attack turned out not to be about protection but about a show of force, progressives who supported the war felt duped. And as the Iraq war ended and was replaced with an occupation, it became even less about protection, and progressives have been calling for a pullout—to *protect* the troops.

The conservative idea of strong security at home is based on a justice system that inflicts harsh punishment on criminals—another example of a show of force. Punishment is required to enforce discipline, and that's why conservatives advocate for policies like three-strikes laws.

Progressive security is based on nurturance, so domestic protection takes on a very different form. The best way to prevent crime is not harsh deterrence—at least in the case of the death penalty, this clearly does not work. Instead, security comes from the broad application of progressive principles.

Crime is lower when poverty is lower, so ensuring secure communities requires providing opportunity and a decent living for all its members—extensions of the "human dignity principle." Therefore, broad prosperity is crucial to security.

The "common good principle" requires that secure communities come from having a well-funded infrastructure. This means funding not only police and fire departments but also departments like FEMA, the Army Corps of Engineers, the National Weather Service, and a public health infrastructure—as well as good schools and universal health care. Thus, a strong infrastructure is crucial to security.

So security looks like all the other contested concepts we have discussed. Progressives and conservatives have different points of view as to what security—and the related values of strength and protection—means, and the difference in meaning comes from their different views of the world.

In this chapter, we've articulated the basic progressive values. The discussion of each value should have shown that it's not enough just to say "equality" or "responsibility" in a speech, because conservatives and progressives each have their own understanding of what these values mean. You have to talk about *your* understanding of each of these words. Doing so allows progressives to reclaim the values that have been co-opted by conservatives and advance our vision for America.

7

STRATEGIC INITIATIVES

Thinking, from a progressive standpoint, is more than just reasoning step-by-step, or articulating a worldview, or using frames and metaphors. The most powerful form of thinking is *strategic*. It is not just a matter of thinking ahead. It is matter of changing the landscape of thought and action. It is a matter of setting many things in motion by setting one thing in motion. It is a matter of reconfiguring the future by doing one thing in the present. Conservatives have been very good at strategic thinking. Progressives have not.

Strategic initiatives are policy proposals in one area that have an impact far beyond the explicit change promoted. They can be classified into two types. The first is the *multifaceted* initiative, where a targeted policy change has far-reaching effects across many areas. It advances a range of goals through one change.

For instance, *tax cuts* constitute a conservative multifaceted strategic initiative. They are not simply about lowering taxes. They are a kill-all-birds-with-one-stone approach to getting rid of social programs and protective or regulatory government oversight—an overarching goal of the conservative movement.

Another multifaceted conservative strategic initiative is "tort reform," which has been made to sound like it is just about capping large damage awards and lawyers' fees. It is really a destruction of the civil justice system's capacity to deter corporations from acts that harm the public, since it is the lawyers' fees that permit the system to function. Moreover, if successful, it will also dry up one of the major sources of campaign finance for progressive candidates, which comes from trial lawyers.

On the progressive side, investment in renewable energy is a multifaceted strategic initiative for better environmental policy, increased security, job creation, Third World development, and economic stimulation. George Lakoff has discussed this in detail in *Don't Think of an Elephant!*[1]

A second type of strategic initiative is the *domino* initiative. Such policy changes are meant as a first step toward a broader goal, where the next steps are easier or inevitable. So called partial-birth abortion is a conservative domino initiative to ban abortion. School vouchers are a similar ploy toward eventually privatizing the education system and giving religious schools public funding and a major educational role. President Bush vetoed the stem cell research bill because he saw it as a first step down a slippery slope to the acceptance of abortion.

Conservative strategic initiatives have one critical component: Their ultimate goals are typically not explicit. So when conservative leaders discuss "tax relief," they rarely say that their ultimate goal is to get rid of progressive government and eliminate social programs. These strategic goals are typically framed in private, in the confines of think tanks, policy sessions, and strategy talks. Thus, the Cato Institute published an article in 1983 on privatizing Social Security.[2] Though the proposal was far from secret, public discussion of creating private accounts are framed as ways to protect Social Security, when the real goal is to destroy it.

But there is a bright side to the need for such deception. It tells us that Americans are *too progressive* to endorse the strategic ends of tax cuts and privatization. Americans do not want to see government stripped of its public interest functions. That is why

a lot of conservative strategic initiatives have *covert* goals—
because most Americans will not support them.

Instead, they couch their initiatives in positive terms, like tax
initiatives in terms of "tax relief." Conservatives frame the initiative as helping individuals, giving them back their money so
they can spend it how they see fit. In a sense, tax relief is framed
as a progressive policy: government helping and showing compassion for the public.

One way for progressives to counter such hidden agendas is
to discuss them openly. We need to get beyond how conservatives
are framing the issues publicly and point out their real goals.

And there's no bigger current issue than the Iraq war to
show how a strategic initiative of the conservatives is framed in
progressive terms and hides a much longer-term conservative
agenda.

THE IRAQ WAR

As with tax cuts, there was an explicit justification for the invasion of Iraq that is well known. It was the primary frame of the
war discourse:

- Find and destroy the weapons of mass destruction.
- Oust Saddam Hussein and free the Iraqi people to es-
  tablish their own democracy.
- Allow Iraqi businessmen to establish a free market.
- Use the profits from Iraqi oil to build the infrastructure
  for the people of Iraq.
- Allow Iraq to become a shining example of liberty, free
  markets, and democracy in the Middle East.

Those are all generally *progressive* goals, which explains the broad
support of the Iraq invasion. Americans wanted to believe we

were doing good, we were promoting an open and free society, we were showing our *empathy* for Iraqis. After all, it is progressives who champion international aid, the protection of human rights, and the ideal that the proceeds of a country's resources should go to the people of that country. The Bush administration framed the Iraq invasion in terms of a humanitarian mission in order to gain the support of progressives and biconceptuals.

However, as with "tax relief," there are strategic goals of the Iraq adventure that are not often publicly stated but many progressives have understood. It is because of these strategic goals, and the realization that the humanitarian goals either could not be achieved or would take a backseat to the strategic goals, that many progressives opposed the Iraq invasion. Among the Bush administration's strategic goals of the Iraq invasion:

- Show that the global order can be reshaped to our advantage by military means, and show enough force to intimidate other countries in the Middle East.
- Use the war—linked to the "war on terror"—as a way to establish domestic war powers and much greater political control in the United States for the president and the administration.
- Shift domestic spending from social programs to the military, and shift domestic wealth and power to defense contractors and the oil industry.
- Establish a controllable "client state" government in Iraq.
- Gain access to the world's second-largest oil reserve.
- Establish permanent military bases in the heart of the Middle East to gain a strategic position, particularly with regard to Iran.
- Use the war as a rallying call for electoral advantage in America.
- Allow American corporations to take control of a significant portion of Iraq's economy.

- Privatize military functions in order to (a) maximize the effect of fighting forces, (b) increase profits for military contractors, and (c) remove accountability from the military for such actions as torture and bribery.
- Establish the dominance and independence of the United States in world affairs by ignoring the will of many of our NATO allies and the UN.

None of those is a progressive goal, which is why the war proponents do not often state them. Americans are just too progressive to accept them. However, many of these goals can be found in think tank publications and right-wing magazines. Many of the architects of the war—Vice President Dick Cheney, Defense Secretary Donald Rumsfeld, World Bank President and former undersecretary for defense Paul Wolfowitz, U.S. Ambassador to Iraq Zalmay Khalilzad, I. Lewis Libby (former chief of staff for Cheney), William Kristol (editor of *The Weekly Standard*), and Governor Jeb Bush of Florida, among others—explicitly endorsed such an agenda as part of the Project for the New American Century in 1997.[3]

If we recognize that these strategic goals are the important focus of the Iraq invasion, then what we see in Iraq is not "incompetence," as has been the pervasive criticism from progressives.[4] The conservative architects of the war, and those in charge, were less interested in the humanitarian mission of the war than in these strategic goals.

Progressives have generally fallen into the "laundry list trap," choosing limited policy initiatives and acting issue by issue, advancing a host of specific programs, none of which highlight—or are articulated as promoting—our values. Unlike conservatives, we have no multifaceted strategic initiatives with far-reaching consequences.

And because we act program by program and issue by issue, we have failed to come together as a movement. Environmentalists, labor unions, feminists, health-care activists, consumer advocates, immigrants' advocates, etc., all work on their own programs, all have their own funders, their own publications, their own lobbyists, and so on.

The issues and programs these groups advance are extremely important, but by acting alone, each of them—and all of us—is losing.

We can win, if we act strategically. We must begin to identify multifaceted initiatives that are long-term, that work across issues, that unify progressive groups and the grass roots, and that express our common values and advance all of our goals simultaneously. And we can act on these initiatives at the federal level, the state level, the regional level, or the local level.

And unlike conservatives, we can act strategically, without hiding our strategic goals. Our initiatives broadly advance the common good. You will not find us trying to dismantle government, or increase American hegemony, or diminish the common good.

While there are many progressive strategic initiatives we can all rally behind, we will look at four possibilities by way of example: clean elections, healthy food, ethical business, and transit-for-all. Our goal here is not to be prescriptive and offer a list of legislative measures to advance these initiatives; we discuss these to illustrate how the initiatives can be far-reaching, how they might promote progressive values, and how they offer an opportunity for progressives to collaborate and work together as a movement.

CLEAN ELECTIONS

Most Americans are aware that politics is dirty and that what makes it so is the corrupting influence of money. The recent DeLay-Abramoff scandal is just the latest of many reminders. David Sirota's *Hostile Takeover* is a guidebook on how corporations use political donations as investments in largesse from the government.[5] Our campaign finance system—a system of legalized bribery and quid pro quo—is primarily to blame.

Most politicians—conservative or progressive—have paid lip service to the idea of "campaign finance reform," because they know Americans want it. But a host of legislative measures in Congress have only tinkered around the edges. Some have been mildly successful, while others have failed. It may be time for progressives to seize the opportunity to put their strongest support behind a crucial strategic initiative: clean elections.

The idea is simple: Provide full public financing of elections for qualified candidates. That is, give candidates who have established a broad base of community support a grant to run their campaigns. If candidates accept public funds, they must agree to forgo any private contributions.

Clean elections grants *equal opportunity* to run for public office. It ensures that elections are *fair* by stripping away the corrosive influence of money. Elections are a *public good* and should be supported by the common wealth.

Clean elections has far-reaching consequences beyond limiting campaign spending and curbing corruption—it's been called the "reform that makes all other reforms possible." It hits on almost every political issue because it impacts the basic functioning of our government.

Clean elections actually *saves the public money*—lots of it. Although there is a cost to the program, far more money is saved because elected officials will no longer use public funds to pay back their donors many times over—sometimes hundreds or thousands of times over—for their electoral contributions. The paybacks are in the form of subsidies, no-bid contracts, pork, regulation changes, tax breaks, and so on—all ways the special interests feed at the public trough. There may be no better way to cut government spending on corporate giveaways—vast transfers of wealth from the public treasury to wealthy stockholders. The public gains by not losing.

Another way the public gains is in the area of proposals that serve the public good but not the corporate good. When progressive groups fight for change—no matter how popular or public-spirited their proposals are—their reforms are typically met with staunch resistance in Congress (or in statehouses or city councils) because industries invest in our elected officials to stop these proposals.

If we want universal health care, we need to end the influence of HMOs and drug companies. If we want sane environmental policy, we need to turn off the campaign finance spigot from the oil, timber, coal, nuclear power, mineral, and agribusiness industries. If we want a living wage and acceptable labor standards for workers, we need to eliminate the money pipeline from big business to lawmakers. If we want sustainable development in our communities, we need to stem the flow of cash from real estate developers, who are almost always the biggest contributors in local politics.

If we want local, state, and national budgets that reflect the priorities of the public—money for schools, transit, health care, parks, etc.—we need to end the influence of all special interests that undermines the will of the people. If we want a balanced budget and sane fiscal policy, we must end the massive corporate subsidies that result from campaign contributions. If we want to have our elected officials do their jobs, instead of spending their time raising money for their next election, we need to end the fund-raising rat race. If we want more candidates, and a more diverse range of candidates, we need to end the disparities in fund-raising ability.

We can do this all with clean elections.

HEALTHY FOOD

A fundamental responsibility of government is to advance the common good. For instance, we expect government to keep our water systems clean, so that we have potable running water. We expect government to manage and preserve our forests and parks, so that our children may enjoy Earth's natural wonders. We expect government to regulate the production of drugs, so that pharmaceuticals are safe. While the realities can fall short of these expectations, these are nevertheless the goals we seek.

Our expectations should be no less for our food.

Unfortunately, our government is shirking this responsibility. It is supporting the production of commodity agriculture—plants that are typically used in processed foods manufactured primarily by large companies. These processed foods have few nutrients and lots of empty calories, and are contributing to an obesity epidemic. What's worse, government subsidies help to make commodity and processed foods cheaper and more accessible than fresh produce and wholesome foods.

We are in the midst of a food crisis.

This is a crisis in which the federal government has had a very active role. For instance, the federal government spends more than $20 billion a year to subsidize the production of cheap commodity corn.[6] This creates an overabundance of inedible corn that is the raw material in processed foods. The corn is turned into a variety of products, like high-fructose corn syrup, or fed to maltreated animals on factory farms that are slaughtered for cheap meat.

Further subsidies go into the production of other commodity crops—generally grown by large industrial farms—like wheat, cotton, soybeans, feed grains, and tobacco. Often, it is proxy owners—not the farmers who work the land—who reap the benefit of these subsidies. Agribusinesses like Archer Daniels Midland and Cargill are rewarded with a cheap supply of commodity products, subsidized by the government, to turn into processed foods. Industrial agriculture—a petroleum-heavy process—also gets the added benefit of cheap oil, subsidized to the tune of billions of dollars each year.

Adding insult to injury, taxpayers are expected to pick up the tab for "externalization" of costs in industrial agriculture— cleaning up contaminated water systems from pesticide runoff; treating obesity, diabetes, and other food-related diseases; cleaning up air pollution from intense tilling or from fertilizers; and disposing of waste.

Government policy has a lot to do with the types and quality of food we have access to. It's time we begin to redirect this system with a healthy foods initiative.

This initiative requires one major change in government policy: Shift the massive subsidies that currently find their way to agribusiness and use that taxpayer money to create the infrastructure for a healthy, affordable food system. This will not happen overnight; it is a long-term initiative that could eventually bring us a sustainable agricultural system.

Let's make a compact with America's farmers, ranchers, fishermen, and all others who feed us from nature's bounty. In exchange for growing healthy food for our communities and protecting the sanctity of our earth and our commons for future generations, we will invest in sustainable farming. This can be done on a local and regional level (as it has initially grown), on a state level, or on a national level.[7]

This may be done in many ways. We can provide tax credits for farmers who reduce their dependency on pesticides and herbicides, which would get rid of the cancer-causing chemicals in our food. Our tax policy can be structured to promote family farm ownership, rather than absentee and corporate ownership. When farms are family-owned, there is a vested interest and pride taken in the quality of the food and the management of the local ecosystem. We could subsidize the creation of land trusts for farmers and ranchers who sustainably manage the land. We can invest in community gardens, to provide a space for growing food in urban areas. In fact, many current government policies could stay the same, except that the loans and subsidies would guarantee a price for food grown sustainably. Government could have an enormous impact in reducing the cost of and increasing access to healthy, locally grown, organic, and sustainable foods.

The above suggestions are offered only as various possibilities. This is a strategic initiative that all progressives should rally around to figure out how best to work toward it. It's about *protection*: The government should make sure we have healthy food. It's about *equality*: Good and healthy food should not be a luxury reserved for the rich. It's about *diversity*: having a polyculture system and distinctive varieties of food. It's an expansion of *freedom*: Everyone should have access to good food. It's using the *common wealth for the common good* to promote public health and increase quality of life.

The benefits of such a strategic initiative do not end there.

It will have positive consequences for public health. Processed food and fast-food chains are making us unhealthy and fat. This is particularly true in low-income and minority communities. Because of food-related illnesses, the current generation of children is the first generation in American history that will likely have *shorter* life spans than their parents.[8] So a healthy foods initiative is a *class issue*, a *race issue*, and a *public health issue*.

Industrial agriculture also requires massive inputs of petroleum, erodes the soil, uses excessive amounts of water, and contaminates the air and water systems through the use of chemicals, to name a few consequences. So a healthy foods initiative is an *environmental issue* and a *foreign policy issue*. If we changed our food production system, we could greatly reduce our dependency on foreign oil.

Such a strategic initiative would also support and promote local, neighborhood-based farmers' markets—which are great places to enjoy quality food and build community. They also create bonds between urban centers and surrounding rural communities. So a healthy foods initiative is a *civics issue* and a *quality-of-life issue*.

The impact of agricultural subsidies doesn't end at our nation's borders, however. Much of our surplus of commodity crops is sold overseas, for below-market prices (because it is subsidized). This has forced many subsistence farmers off their land because they cannot compete with the subsidized prices. Ironically, these subsidies have contributed to both obesity and hunger (as Michael Pollan has pointed out)[9]—making us fat while starving foreigners. Without other opportunities, these farmers have had to leave their lands in search of work. But little awaits, so they have emigrated, many to the United States. Thus, a healthy foods initiative is also a *world hunger issue*, a *poverty issue*, an *economic issue*, and an *immigration issue*.

Finally, the move toward industrial monoculture—growing only one crop on a farm—has increased the size of farms and their efficiency (in terms of laborers per acre, not necessarily food production per acre). This has caused an exodus from our rural communities. Additionally, the homogeneity of our agriculture puts us at a security risk. When we plant so much of one crop and raise animals in close confines, a change in weather from year to year (say, because of a climate crisis) or a disease (avian flu, mad cow disease) could wipe out much of our food supply. By diversifying, we can better protect our food system. So healthy food is a *rural vitality issue* and a *security issue*.

A healthy foods initiative can also unify us as progressives. It can bring together environmentalists, labor activists, fair trade proponents, social justice advocates, civil rights activists, and many others.

ETHICAL BUSINESS

The market is a tool to enhance the common good. As we saw in Chapter 5, failure to meet this expectation is rightly perceived as market failure. The rules that govern the market should create incentives to enhance the common good, but they should also punish violations of the common good.

Unfortunately, the current charters of corporations—a legal privilege given to business—strays far from this expectation. Corporations' foremost aim is to maximize profit for their shareholders. This creates incentives to lower labor costs, provide fewer health-care benefits, push environmental laws to their limits, and externalize as many costs as possible. The only real incentive for a corporation to act for the common good is if it is perceived as good for business. This usually means for public relations purposes—if charity or community works provide good PR, they should be done.

This is not to say all corporations are evil. Indeed, many corporations are good and provide excellent and essential services for the public. And many people working for those corporations are public-spirited and rightly see their mission in business as enhancing the common good. But all too often, corporations violate the public interest because they can be *legally required to do so*. If managers do not maximize corporate profit, they may be sued by their shareholders.

It does not have to work this way. There are two general approaches to ethical business. One is to leave the corporate model essentially intact but to alter the rules and landscape of the market in which corporations act. This idea, put forth by Working Assets founder Peter Barnes, is to assign all Americans property rights to the commons—through an air trust, an ocean trust, watershed trusts, soil trusts, an Internet trust, an electromagnetic spectrum trust—and charge businesses for the use of the commons (which, currently, are usually given away for free). For instance, to slow global warming, an air trust would give a certain amount of greenhouse gas credits every year, and businesses would have to bid for these credits. Every year, the spigot would be turned down, allowing fewer greenhouse gases to be put in our atmosphere. This would create incentives to reduce global warming—contributing to it would eventually become costly. The money raised from this system could be used to clean up our atmosphere and invest in renewable energy.

Like the Federal Reserve, these trusts would be managed by federally appointed trustees, insulated from political pressures, to protect our common wealth for the public interest and for future generations. The trustees would have a fiduciary responsibility to leave, in the words of John Locke, "as much, and as good" for others, including our children.[10]

The money generated from these trusts can be used to clean up our air, invest in renewable-energy technology, provide job training and placement assistance for people who have lost their jobs from outsourcing, or a whole host of other projects to promote the common good. This is the idea advanced by Barnes in his new book, *Capitalism 3.0*.[11]

The other approach to ethical business is corporate rechartering, writing into the governing structure of corporations an interest for *stakeholders*—citizens, workers, communities, ecosystems, etc., who are greatly impacted by what a corporation does but do not necessarily own corporate stock. A corporation would have to renew its charter every so often, say, every ten years. To be renewed, a corporation would have to demonstrate its commitment to stakeholders and to social responsibility. Therefore, a corporation would not have to sacrifice the interests of its stakeholders to eke out greater profit margins for its shareholders. To demonstrate this commitment, a corporation might raise wages, clean up a local ecosystem, take steps to reduce pollution, support local sports teams, and so on.

A strategic initiative could take either of the above approaches or contain a little of both. Such an initiative would advance the progressive idea of the *common good* and counter the conservative notion of the "free market." Like other strategic initiatives, it brings progressives of all stripes together. It's a *labor issue*, giving workers a legal stake in business. It's an *environmental issue*, changing the rules of the market so that business does no harm to the commons. It's a *community issue*, promoting the notion that businesses should enhance the communities where they are located and which they serve. And it's a *health issue*, because reducing pollution means better health.

TRANSIT-FOR-ALL

The way we move shapes almost everything about our nation. Our dependence on cars pollutes the environment, harms our personal health, restricts social and economic mobility, and chains us to foreign oil. With one multifaceted change over the course of many years, a "transit-for-all" initiative can help slay all of these beasts. Simply put, the idea is to take the $70 billion a year that currently goes to subsidizing cheap oil—the essential ingredient of our car culture—and shift it toward building and promoting public transit systems. Additional funding could come from the over $250 billion a year that is currently spent on building and maintaining the highway infrastructure.

Transit-for-all means expanding and improving public transportation at the local, regional, and federal levels. It means investing in bus and light rail in urban areas to create clean, convenient, reliable, and accessible webs of transportation. It means making our city cores more bike- and pedestrian-friendly. It means expanding commuter rail, to connect urban and suburban centers typically served by car transportation. It means investing in high-speed rail, to move people, goods, and services from city to city. Moving within urban cores and connecting urban and suburban hubs, these webs would extend to all auto-dense areas.

Transit-for-all is about values. Improving public transportation is about giving all Americans the *freedom* of *equal access* to social and economic *opportunities* that enhance our *quality of life*. Investing in alternative transportation is using the *common wealth for the common good*. It is an *expansion of freedom*, creating more *diverse* transportation.

Transit-for-all is a progressive strategic initiative to advance many of our goals at once.

It's an *economic issue*. It would increase mobility of goods and labor. It would revitalize neglected neighborhoods. And it would spur growth and attract development.

It's a *labor issue*. It would create many jobs—construction workers, engineers, bus drivers, rail operators, administrators, ticket vendors. Many of these jobs are sustainable union jobs. An increase of union jobs empowers labor to negotiate better contracts and helps develop better conditions for workers throughout the community.

It's an *environmental issue*. By now the relationship between fossil fuels and the environment is well understood and accepted. Burning oil releases into the atmosphere greenhouse gases that destabilize the climate. Mass transit reduces society's dependence on oil and helps remediate some of the dangers of global warming.

It's a *public health issue*. Our air quality is abysmal and getting worse. The dirty exhaust from cars is driving an air pollution crisis that increases health hazards and claims tens of thousands of American lives, not to mention millions of dollars, every year.[12] And no one needs to be reminded of the physical, emotional, and economic damage of six million annual auto accidents. Better public transportation helps us transition out of this dirty and dangerous technology. In doing so, it could rescue millions of

Americans from debilitating health problems and even death—
and save the public from bearing the burden of preventable medical expenses.

It's a *national security issue.* Kicking our oil habit not only
benefits human and environmental health, it secures our nation.
Greater energy autonomy frees us from our dangerous dependence on a volatile region.

With a transit-for-all initiative, laborers, economists, environmentalists, and security buffs could walk under the same
banner. An investment in a transit-for-all strategic initiative is
an investment in freedom, health, the economy, and national security.

It is time for progressives to start thinking strategically. The
most effective long-term strategies start with the most commonplace activities: eating, traveling to work, and working in a business. Home is where we live. Start there.

8

THE ART OF ARGUMENTS

Let's see how it all fits together: The moral worldviews, visions, values, principles, frames, and language all come together in political arguments. As we look at arguments, we find certain characteristics common to all effective and successful arguments:

- They have moral premises, that is, they are about what is right.
- They use versions of contested values taken from a particular moral worldview.
- They have an implicit or explicit narrative structure, i.e., they all tell stories with heroes, villains, victims, common themes, etc.
- They also serve as counterarguments: They undermine arguments on the other side.
- They have issue-defining frames that set up the problem and the solution.
- They use commonplace frames—frames known so widely that they resonate immediately, whether true or not.
- They use language with surface frames that evoke deeper frames.

None of this should be surprising. Rhetoricians have long been aware of such details. But it is important that *you* know how all this works so you can use the knowledge.

OBAMA ON THE ESTATE TAX

For a close look at a successful argument, let's review statements by Senator Barack Obama of Illinois on the proposed repeal of the estate tax, posted on his Web site on June 7, 2006.[1]

First of all, let's call this trillion-dollar giveaway what it is—the Paris Hilton Tax Break. It's about giving billions of dollars to billionaire heirs and heiresses at a time when American taxpayers just can't afford it. . . .

I'm eager for the American people to choose. Because if people want their government to spend one trillion dollars—an amount more than double what we've spent on Iraq, Afghanistan, and the War on Terror combined—on tax breaks for multimillionaires and multibillionaires, then the Republican Party is your party.

If the American people want to borrow billions more from the Chinese, spend billions more in taxes to pay the interest on our debt, and watch billions cut from health care and education and Gulf Coast Reconstruction, then the Paris Hilton Tax Break is your tax break.

This isn't about saving small businesses and family farms. We can reform the estate tax to protect these Americans. We can set it at a level where no small business or family farm is ever affected—and we can do it in a way that doesn't cost us a trillion dollars. In fact, we've offered to reform the estate tax in this way time and time again. . . .

I would ask the American people one question. At a time like this—a time where America finds itself deeply in debt, struggling to pay for a war in Iraq, a war in Afghanistan, security for our homeland, armor for our troops, health care for our workers, and education for our children—at a time of all this need, can you imagine opening *Forbes* magazine, looking at their list of the 400 wealthiest Americans, and realizing that our government gave the people on that list over a trillion dollars' worth of tax breaks?

I know I can't imagine that. And I would bet that most Americans can't imagine that either. So if the Republicans want to bring up their Paris Hilton Tax Break to use it as an election issue later, I say go for it. Because I can think of no better statement about where and how we differ in priorities than that.

There is a lot going on in those remarks that is worth looking at closely. What makes this a good progressive argument is its moral vision and political principles. First, there is *empathy*, a concern for the nation, for the safety of our soldiers, for the health of our workers, and for the education of our children. Second, there is the understanding of taxation in terms of the principle of using the *common wealth for the common good*—a health-care system for all and an educational system in need of funding.

Obama also invokes the commonplace knowledge about money, using the *economic equivalence frame*: Two economic actions with the same initial state and the same result are equivalent. Obama uses two instances of this.

1. Not to collect the estimated trillion dollars under the present estate tax is the equivalent of giving a trillion dollars of taxpayers' money to wealthy heirs and heiresses.

2. Not spending a trillion dollars of taxpayers' money where it is desperately needed by U.S. citizens is the equivalent of taking a trillion dollars from those citizens in desperate need.

Putting 1 and 2 together, we get 3 as a consequence.

3. Either spend a trillion dollars of taxpayers' money on the desperate needs of U.S. citizens or give those trillion dollars to wealthy heirs and heiresses.

His argument sets up an issue-defining frame: What is the estate tax?

American millionaires and billionaires will pay half of their accumulated millions and billions—and only after they are dead! The other half of the millions and billions will go to their heirs—the Paris Hiltons of the country—who did not earn it.

Question: What should we, the taxpayers, do with the trillion dollars owed to us? Should we put it into a health and educational infrastructure to benefit millions of the most needy and hardworking of our citizens? Or should we turn our backs on them and just give it away to the heirs who want *all*, not just half, of the millions and billions they didn't earn?

That is the issue; the answer is built in to the question.

If you have empathy, a commitment to the common good, and a sense of fairness, the answer is clear: As the fairness principle dictates, you should get what you deserve. Hardworking, needy people deserve the schools and hospitals those dollars can provide more than the heirs who didn't earn the money and who will get half of it anyway.

Obama's statements also use a narrative structure, complete with heroes and villains: Ending the estate tax is a threat to the most vulnerable people—taking away money for what they desperately need. They are the victims. The villains are those who would take it from them—conservative legislators and some of the nation's wealthiest families, who have spent tens of millions to lobby for the repeal of this tax. The hero, the rescuer, is you, the voter, who can change the course of the nation. Persuade your legislators to vote for what is moral, and turn them out of office if they refuse to do the right thing.

The inferences are the point of the speech, and he lays them out explicitly: Keeping the estate tax allows us to use our trillion dollars where it is most needed—on our health and education infrastructure and on protecting our troops—instead of giving it away to people who neither need it nor deserve it.

You—citizen, taxpayer, voter—can rescue tens of millions of worthy and needy people from the clutches of villainous conservatives who want to transfer a trillion dollars from the common wealth of hardworking Americans to wealthy individual heirs and heiresses who didn't earn it and don't need it.

Finally, Obama's remarks are carefully constructed to undermine the arguments of conservatives, who frame the social programs funded by taxation as government handouts to the undeserving. Obama flips the taxes-as-handouts frame on its head, to yield a frame in which tax breaks are handouts to the rich, and the estate tax is a transfer of wealth from ordinary taxpayers to wealthy individuals—a frame that tells a vital truth.

It is worth noting that this argument is not a perfect progressive argument. The "common good principle" has two parts, and this argument hits the first. Implicitly invoking the fact that the common wealth can serve the common good only when wealth is in the hands of the commons (and not the individual) is important. However, so is the notion that the opportunities afforded by the common wealth are what allow the accumulation of personal wealth. As such, everyone has a responsibility to repay the common wealth proportional to the benefits he or she derived from it. This part of the common good principle is missing from Obama's argument.

Nevertheless, Obama's remarks have the basic elements of a political argument that can be applied to all sorts of progressive issues besides the estate tax: the graduated income tax; the auctioning of the airwaves; the giving away or cheap sale of timber, mineral, and grazing rights on public lands; the privatization of public lands; and private property rights vs. the environment.

The main concern of the frame is that money be kept in the common wealth (or the hands of the government) in order to be used for the common good.

HOW ARGUMENT FRAMES WORK

Let's take a step back and look at the general argument frame, which, in addition to the values and structure elements detailed above, shapes the progressive stance on the estate tax. Remember, frames are not simply about words. Frames are the mental structures by which we understand and interact with the world. In fact, frames can be constructed using other frames (as argument frames are). The general argument frame includes *moral values*, *fundamental principles*, *issue-defining frames*, *commonplace frames*, *surface frames*, and *inferences*. Argument frames apply to many issues. Depending on the issue-defining frame that's "plugged in," you can use the same argument frame across many issue areas.

For instance, let's look at the common wealth for the common good frame:

Moral values: Empathy and responsibility. We care about people and have a responsibility to act on that care.

Fundamental principles: (a) The common good—individual goals depend upon the use of the common wealth for the common good. (b) Fairness—it is unfair to take economic resources from the commons and transfer them to wealthy individuals who don't need them.

Issue-defining frame: The estate tax (other issues, as mentioned above, can fit here).

Commonplace frame: The economic equivalence frame. Not taking in money owed is economically equivalent to giving it away. Not giving money to those owed is economically equivalent to taking it away.

Inference: To protect the common good, we must maintain the common wealth.

Functioning as a progressive or conservative means having a stock of general argument frames that are used not just on one issue but on many issues. That is why someone attuned to politics can immediately understand or construct a "new" argument as soon as a new issue arises. The "new" argument is not really new at all. It is an instance of a general argument frame with a new issue-defining frame plugged in, and sometimes a new commonplace frame or surface frame. But the overall structure and content of the argument remain the same. We'll get to more of these argument frames in a moment, but first a bit needs to be said about the components of an argument frame.

Commonplace frames are used to understand how the world works. Some are relatively accurate. Some are grossly inaccurate. But, accurate or inaccurate, they are used in political arguments. It is important to recognize them for three reasons: so you're not taken in by the false ones, so you can recognize and counter them, and so you can factor them out to see the more general argument frame. They can be very general, that is, applying across many issue areas, or they can be relatively specific, having bearing on only one or several issues.

Commonplace frames are not a matter of moral values, or fundamental principles, or issue-defining frames, or even surface frames. They are taken as a matter of common knowledge or common sense. They can sometimes be picked out and discussed

consciously, and ridiculed and undermined when they are false
or ridiculous.

Let's look at some commonplace frames that are often used in
political arguments.

Bad apple frame. Consider the saying "A bad apple spoils the
barrel." The implication is that if you remove the bad apple or
some small number of bad apples, the others will be fine. The rot
is localized and will not spread. Rot here is a metaphor for immorality. In a case where there is immoral behavior, it points
blame at one person or a few people—and not to any broader
systemic immorality, an immoral policy, or an immoral culture.

This commonplace frame has been used to limit the inquiry
into torture as a systemic problem in the military (as in the Abu
Ghraib scandal), so the problem is contained. The army just got
rid of the "bad apples"—the lowest-ranking military personnel
involved. The same was true of Enron Corporation, where a few
executives (Jeffrey Skilling and Kenneth Lay) were identified as
bad apples, rather than the entire culture of Enron, where top-
level and even midlevel employees commonly schemed to rip off
the public by taking advantage of the deregulation of utilities
with illegal actions like those code-named "Death Star" and
"Get Shorty."

Tradition is right frame. This frame says that if some idea or institution has "passed the test of time," then it is right. This is
used in arguments against allowing gays and lesbians to marry,
where it is argued that marriage has traditionally been between a
man and a woman, and therefore that is the right position to
take on the question. A related argument is the commonplace
Voters are Right frame, used against gay marriage on the grounds
that, since legislatures in many states have passed laws to this effect, it is right.

Teenage minimum wage frame. This frame is quite specific and
claims that most people working at the minimum wage are
teenagers in their first jobs (say, as grocery store baggers) who are

supported by their parents. This is then used to argue against raising the minimum wage, which would kill off entry-level jobs since wages will be too high. Both are false, but the commonplace frame is widely accepted.

Adaptation frame. This frame occurs quite often. It says that if some phenomenon is natural or pervasive, you can't overcome it and may as well accept it and adapt as well as possible. Liberals use it to argue for legalizing marijuana: People are naturally going to smoke pot, just like they're going to drink alcohol, and you may as well legalize it. Liberals also use it in supporting sex education: People are going to have sex anyway, so the best thing to do is to educate them on safe practices and birth control methods. Safe abortion advocates also use the adaptation frame: Many women with unwanted pregnancies always have, and will, get abortions, so it's best to make abortion safe and legal. Mayor Michael Bloomberg of New York has argued that immigrants are going to go where they can find work, so border walls won't keep them from entering the country.

Slippery slope frame. There is a point on a scale where everything appears to be fine. But there is also some force or tendency operating so that moving a short distance farther on the scale will lead to more and more movement in the same direction until either a disaster happens or something ludicrous results. This is used in reductio ad absurdum arguments against apparently small changes in a given direction.

For example, conservatives have been known to argue that if the minimum wage is to be raised from $5.15 to $7 an hour, why not $10 an hour or $100 an hour? Anti–gay marriage conservatives argue that if gays and lesbians are allowed to marry, the next thing will be people wanting to marry dogs. Asked about President Bush's veto of the stem cell research bill, Tony Snow, the White House press secretary, replied that the president didn't want to move along the slippery slope to permitting the killing of living human beings.

Prototype frames. Among the most important of the common-place frames are the prototype frames, where you reason about a category on the basis of some subcategory (real or imagined). The best known is the social stereotype. For instance, both conservatives and progressives use stereotypes of immigrants, though very different ones. One stereotype is that they are "illegals"— felons who don't speak English, are uneducated and uneducable, take jobs away from Americans, use up local funding for education and health, and who, as criminals, are not to be trusted. This is common in conservative arguments. Another stereotype, common in progressive arguments, is the "undocumented worker"—the honest, hardworking, good family man or woman, doing essential work that Americans don't want to do for low pay, making our lifestyles possible, and seeking to find the American dream, just like Americans.

Many categories have prototypes for typical cases (used for reasoning about the category in the absence of other knowledge), ideal cases (setting standards for evaluation), and nightmare cases (to be avoided at all costs). President Bush projects the typical American male stereotype—well meaning, sincere and straightforward, religious, friendly and folksy, not overly well educated, but strong, strict, and in charge when he has to be. Progressives tend to see him as the nightmare president: stupid, ignorant, and incompetent; mean, greedy, selfish, and corrupt; arrogant, authoritarian, and unwilling to listen; untrustworthy and underhanded. When the late senator Paul Wellstone of Minnesota was alive, most progressives saw him as the ideal senator: honest, principled, caring, smart, courageous, and strong.

Finally, there are the salient examples, the cases so much on people's minds that they change judgments of probability. Thus, 9/11 is repeated so often as an example of a terrorist attack that people in Omaha, Dayton, and St. Louis think they have a high probability of being attacked by terrorists. Reagan repeated the "welfare queen" example so often that this unusual, indeed unique, example was taken as typical.

In summary, argument frames have the same overall structure. First, there are the moral values and fundamental principles, which both derive from the overall worldview. Then there are the issue-defining and commonplace frames, which exist independent of the overall worldviews but are chosen to fit them. Then there are the surface frames that go with words and slogans. These are chosen to fit all the other frames. And finally, there are the inferences that follow from all these frames.

AMERICAN STORIES

Everybody loves a good story. A good argument includes a story—with heroes and villains. They help transform a set of values, principles, beliefs, and statistics into stories with a beginning, a middle, and an end. Isolated political issues have little appeal. As stories, they begin to connect with a deeper understanding of personal and national identity.

Our most basic roles in narratives are hero, villain, victim, and helper. And some of our basic narrative forms are self-defense (villain hurts hero-victim), rescue (hero, with helpers, fights and wins over villain), overcoming obstacles (hero as victim of circumstance who surmounts difficulties), and achieving potential (hero has special potential and, through discipline and fortitude, achieves it).

Author and former labor secretary Robert Reich identified what he calls the "four essential American stories."[2] The first of these narratives, "The Triumphant Individual," tells the story of the self-made man. With courage, responsibility, and determination, anybody can pull himself up by his own bootstraps. This is the *overcoming-obstacles* narrative. Next, "The Benevolent Society" portrays a collective we're-all-in-this-together effort to better the community. Here society is either a collective hero or the helper to the hero. A more negative story, "The Mob at the

Gates," places America on the top of a moral hierarchy and advocates the urgency of defending the nation against the threats that other nations and peoples pose. Here America is the victim to be protected or rescued. Finally, "Rot at the Top" warns against the evils of powerful elites who abuse their power to the detriment of the common good. Here there is often a collective villain to be fought, though the villain may be a powerful leader.

These narratives, Reich argues, have been repeated so often throughout American history that they have become a part of our culture. Accordingly, employing these narratives helps fashion an argument that resonates with the American public.

These narratives don't just compel the reader, they mold the arguments themselves. They require moral values and fundamental principles to identify heroes, villains, and victims. They require issue-defining frames to tell just what the offenses, rescues, and forms of justice are.

Consider a *kicking-the-habit* narrative. It is a self-defense narrative where addiction is the villain to be overcome. Metaphorically, it is characterized by an undesirable dependence on a detrimental substance (welfare, taxes, fossil fuels, etc.). It is powerful and can destroy the hero-victim. Shedding this dependence requires will and determination. But the fight is internal—the villain is threatening the hero-victim from within.

We acknowledge the power of the substance and sympathize with the addict kicking the habit. We understand that addicts need and deserve help to overcome the problem. Anyone who stands in the way impedes a moral process. Making the story more complex is another simple narrative on top of this. The distributors of the addictive substance are the villains, utterly immoral within this narrative. They are predatory and self-serving (drug dealers, government, oil companies), and their greed would destroy the hero-victim.

In short, narratives give arguments a trajectory that both compels an audience and guides their understanding of the issue itself. To identify the narrative of an argument, start by finding a victim and a villain. What's at stake? Who will rescue the victim and how?

In political life there are ongoing narrative structures. The *culture war* narrative has liberals as the villains (an elite that represents "rot at the top"), ordinary conservatives as the victims, and conservative leaders as the heroes. The "war on terror" is a self-defense narrative, with "the terrorists" as villains. The Iraq war started as self-defense against the evil Saddam Hussein and his weapons of mass destruction. When the weapons were not found, it became a rescue narrative, with the Iraqi people as victims to be rescued from tyranny and provided with democracy.

When it comes to general argument frames used in politics, there are a few basic ones. We will look at two of them here: the "crime-and-punishment frame," used mostly by conservatives, and the "safety-net frame," used mostly by progressives.

THE CRIME-AND-PUNISHMENT FRAME

This frame follows the structure we discussed above and has those same basic elements:

Moral value: Strict father morality—offenses must be punished, or there will be no incentive to avoid future offenses; all order will break down.

Fundamental principle: Moral accounting—justice is retribution. Retribution for an offense should be in proportion to the offense. Justice is, therefore, the appropriately harsh punishment for the offender.

Issue-defining frame: This can be filled with different issues; it is also what allows this argument form to go across issues.

Commonplace frame: (a) Moral essence—extreme or repeat offenses show that the offender is inherently bad. (b) Deterrence—punishment must be harsh to deter future offenses by others.

Inferences: Leniency and mercy remove the incentive to avoid offenses, thus undermining moral values and the very idea of justice. Victims have a right to justice, that is, to harsh sentences for offenders.

Narrative roles: The villains are the offenders. The victims are both the crime victims and members of society in general. The heroes are those who enforce the law.

This frame is used to argue for a great many conservative policies, such as the death penalty, three-strikes laws, mandatory sentencing for drug crimes, treating illegal immigrants as felons, no automatic promotions in public schools, and so on. Let's take a look at three examples (death penalty, three strikes, and standardized testing) of conservative arguments that are instances of this frame, and one example (tort law) of a liberal application of the frame.

Death penalty: Around the world and over millennia, cultures have recognized the basic tenet of a fair justice system: "an eye for an eye" (fundamental principle). If a criminal takes an innocent life, the only fair punishment is to take his or her life in return (moral value). Furthermore, anybody who commits the most serious of crimes—intentionally taking a life—has no chance of reform and no place in society (commonplace frame). If we don't have the courage to uphold justice, we send a dangerous message of leniency to criminals everywhere (commonplace frame).

Three strikes: The logic is simple: If you commit a crime, you go to jail. Individuals need to be held accountable for their actions; sentences need to be proportionate to the crimes (fundamental principle). At a certain point, criminals demonstrate to the public that they can't be reformed (commonplace frame).

They simply have no regard for the laws that structure a stable society (commonplace frame). At this point, society has a duty to say "enough is enough" (moral value). We must protect ourselves by removing repeat offenders: Three strikes and you're out.

Standardized testing: Schools are training grounds for adult life. They teach our sons and daughters the skills they need for the workplace and the work ethic that will ensure their success. The best and the brightest students should be rewarded for hard work, discipline, and scholastic achievement (moral value). Metaphorically, these students are moral people, obeying the law. Tests are both a measure of scholastic achievement and a predictor of future success. Teaching to the test is teaching for success. These tests also provide incentive for the lower-performing students to do better (commonplace frame). Those who repeatedly fail are "breaking the law" and should not be promoted or permitted to graduate—that's their penalty (fundamental principle). Allowing them to pass would undermine the educational system itself, which provides the competition and incentive needed to succeed.

Tort law violations: Interestingly, progressives have adopted the crime-and-punishment frame for tort law violations. Corporations that harm people can be brought to justice through lawsuits in the civil justice system. In such lawsuits, the corporation accused of doing harm—the villain—is the defendant, and the victim is the plaintiff. The trial lawyers are the detectives and prosecutors—the heroes in this story. The funds to support the detective work and prosecution come from the percentage of damages that are paid to the trial lawyers. Corporations can be found "guilty" and are "punished" by having to pay considerable damages.

Incidentally, conservatives are attempting to destroy this system via "tort reform," the capping of damages at levels so low that the attorneys could no longer afford to function as police and prosecutors and the whole system would break down. Their motivation is to make the market "free" from the loss of profit through lawsuits for harming or defrauding the public.

THE SAFETY-NET FRAME

This frame is almost never used by conservatives, while it is quite frequently used by progressives. It also follows the same structure as the crime-and-punishment frame.

Moral values: (a) Empathy and responsibility—we care about people and have a responsibility to act on that care. (b) Freedom—this is primarily freedom from want.

Fundamental principles: (a) Human dignity—there is a baseline of human well-being below which no one should fall in a wealthy, civilized country. (b) The common good—we're all in this together. We all bear responsibility for the nation as a whole.

Issue-defining frame: This can be filled with different issues, like universal health care and minimum wage.

Commonplace frame: The world's wealthiest nation can afford to uphold human dignity.

Inference: This issue (universal health care, minimum wage, etc.) should be handled by government, whose job it is to maximize our inherent freedoms, especially freedom from want. It can—and should—be handled by the government because there is sufficient wealth in the nation as a whole.

Narrative roles: The victims are people vulnerable to falling below the threshold of human dignity. The villains are those who would take away support for them and force indignity upon them. The heroes are citizens who stand up for humane values.

The safety-net frame can be applied to a host of issues, including welfare, corporate responsibility, immigration, Social Security, Medicare, housing for the homeless, the treatment of refugees, pre- and postnatal care, and so on.

If the issue is the status of children of impoverished mothers, the inference is that the government is responsible for seeing that they have enough to eat, a roof over their heads, clothing, immunization shots, and basic health care. Better still, the government should provide reasonable jobs, child care, and transportation so the mothers can earn those things.

Let's take a closer look at three major issues—universal health care, minimum wage, and Social Security—that are compelling cases for the safety-net frame.

Universal health care: Health is the foundation of a full, productive, meaningful life. Without good health, you cannot be what you want to be; you cannot enjoy life to the fullest or be a productive member of society (moral value). Our country was founded on the principle that all Americans have the right to life, liberty, and the pursuit of happiness (fundamental principle). Illness can interfere with all of them—it can bankrupt a family. Illness does not affect only the weak or the aged—illness touches everyone. No one can afford *not* to have adequate health care.

It is our job—as a free, civilized, and wealthy nation—to ensure that our citizens are free from want and needless suffering. A prosperous First World country can afford to guarantee all citizens the right to basic health care and preventive medicine (commonplace frame). Other First World countries do. Health care is not a privilege for those who can afford it (fundamental principle). Because our fundamental freedoms include freedom from want, health care is a basic right. And it is our responsibility as a nation to secure that right for all (moral value).

Minimum wage: "There is a tacit understanding in America—a promise that if you work hard, you should be able to provide for yourself and your family" (commonplace frame).[3] More than thirty million Americans are working hard but living in poverty because we aren't holding up our end of the bargain. In hard times, when the demand for jobs is high, employers can drive down wages below a livable standard. This may create more profits for them or lower consumer prices, but it violates the promise of our nation (fundamental principle). The money America has promised to its workers is going to others—employers and consumers (commonplace frame).

When you can't make a living through hard work, you can lose your home, your dignity, and your stake in society. Raising the minimum wage is a practical thing to do. In states where it has been done, employment has gone up because poor people put their money right back into the economy, creating jobs. But it is also the moral thing to do. It is our moral commitment to our fellow Americans to raise the minimum wage (moral value). To fail to keep the promise of America is to lose the America that has always been a beacon of hope to the world, to lose the America that believes in fair play, and to lose the idea that America, as a wealthy civilized nation, still upholds our basic freedoms, including freedom from want.

Social Security: From deteriorating health to decreased independence, old age is scary. It's even scarier to think about it without necessary financial support (moral value). Our Social Security system guarantees that support; it ensures that the nation doesn't turn its back on hardworking Americans once they reach retirement age. Freedom from want is one of our most cherished freedoms. After a lifetime of dedicated work, it is the government's duty to guarantee that freedom to its elderly, to ensure that its citizens can retire with dignity and not be forced to live in poverty (fundamental principle).

Privatization jeopardizes the very security that Social Security is supposed to guarantee. Inevitably, millions of hardworking Americans who aren't expert investors or who simply have bad luck will wind up losing their lifetime of savings. Their loss will become Wall Street's gain. We must preserve a unified Social Security system and not have the government shirk its responsibility and leave the elderly to play the stock market lottery (commonplace frame).

These arguments all fit the general safety-net frame. But they each require other elements as well. The universal health-care argument uses commonplace knowledge about the effects of ill health. The minimum wage argument uses the knowledge that in states that have raised the minimum wage, jobs have increased; this undercuts the opposition frame, that raising the minimum wage eliminates jobs. The Social Security frame uses two commonplace frames, one about the ravages of old age and one that points out that most people are not expert investors and don't want to risk trying to be.

So we have seen that individual arguments have a general argument frame structure, that political arguments all have a moral basis, that political arguments have the narrative roles of moral stories with heroes and villains, and that the good arguments counter crucial points in the other side's arguments. It is now time to move from arguments to stories.

POLITICAL STORIES AS ARGUMENTS

Perhaps the most effective political arguments come not in the form of arguments but in the form of stories. We have seen that arguments have implicit story elements—heroes, victims, villains, crimes, rewards, punishments. The reverse is also true: Stories have implicit argument elements, the elements in an argument frame. Here is an example of a progressive story, summarized from the Goldman Foundation. The narrative elements in the story include victims, hero, crime, villain, victory, justice, and moral. The story is a self-defense narrative, since the hero is one of the victims. The hero is the "triumphant individual" and the villain represents "rot at the top."

Margie Eugene-Richard [*hero*] grew up in a poor African-American neighborhood in Norco, Louisiana, located between a Shell Chemicals plant and a Motiva oil refinery owned by a Shell subsidiary. The neighborhood was known as "Cancer Alley" because of the very high rates of cancer, birth defects, and other serious health ailments among its residents. [*crime*] Most residents could not afford to move out of the area. [*victims*]

Shell had been buying up property from area residents, many of whom were descendants of sharecroppers and slaves predating the Civil War. There had been some serious accidents at the plant resulting in worker deaths and the release of toxins into the air. [*villain*]

Richard founded Concerned Citizens of Norco in 1989 to seek justice from Shell in the form of fair resettlement costs for her family and neighbors. She collaborated with environmentalists and researchers to release a report that showed that the Shell refinery was releasing more than two million pounds of toxic chemicals into the air each year. She fought court battles and publicly criticized Shell. Her efforts finally led to an investigation by the EPA that faulted Shell for failing to ensure plant safety and for falsifying its emissions reporting. [*victory: hero defeats villain*]

In 2000, mostly due to Richard's efforts, Shell agreed to reduce its emissions by 30 percent, give $5 million for a community development fund, and pay full voluntary relocation costs for neighborhood residents. This was the first community relocation victory in the Deep South and an inspiration for activists battling environmental racism in their own areas. [*justice: hero and victims rewarded; villain punished*]

"Every time we as black Americans stand up for what is right, they say it's for greed of money. It's a fight for longevity," Richard said. "Truth and justice for the betterment of life, the environment and government is the stairway to upward mobility."[4] [*moral*]

THE ART OF ARGUMENTS

We have seen stories of this form countless times. But this is not just a story; it is a political argument. First, it uses the general "community activism frame." Second, it adds to that frame additional commonplace frames that turn it into an environmental justice argument frame.

Here is the argument frame, followed by the additional elements that apply community activism to environmental justice.

- *Argument frame*: Community activism.
- *Moral values*: Empathy (for victims) and responsibility (by hero).
- *Principles*: Common good and human dignity.
- *Value*: Justice.
- *Issue-defining frame*: Pick your favorite activist issue.
- *Commonplace frames*: (a) Criminals should be punished and victims compensated. (b) When community members stand up for themselves, they can win, even against powerful interests. (c) Community leaders who work for the common good and have to overcome severe difficulties to do it should be honored.
- *Inferences*: Those discriminated against should stand up for themselves. Corporations should not trample on the basic human dignity of citizens. Corporations should work for the common good and be held accountable when they harm the public.

Environmental justice additions:

- *Issue-defining frame*: Corporate disregard for a poor minority community is racism. Pollution causes cancer (systemic causation).
- *Inferences*: Racism must be fought. Governmental oversight and regulation should be enforced, and corporations doing wrong should be punished and victims compensated.

In Margie Eugene-Richard's story, we unconsciously and automatically recognize the general narrative structure and the argument frame that we are so familiar with. That is what gives the story its power.

PHOTOS AS STORIES

Like stories, photos can have political content. In particular, they tell stories with political morals and make arguments with political inferences. Consider, for example, the official photograph of President Bush's veto of the stem cell bill (available on the White House Web site at www.whitehouse.gov/news/releases/2006/07/20060719-3.html). He is surrounded by "snowflake babies" and their families. "Snowflake babies" are children who were "adopted" as frozen embryos left over from other families' attempts at in vitro fertilization. They were later born via in vitro fertilization of their "adoptive" mother. There are an estimated four hundred thousand such frozen embryos in America today.

Notice what is "said" by this photo in this context. First, it tells a *rescue* story. If the "snowflake babies" had not been "adopted," they would still be frozen embryos in a freezer somewhere. Worse yet, had the president not vetoed the stem cell research bill, they might have been destroyed as part of a stem cell experiment. The picture connects the children to the frozen "embryos," which are actually blastocysts, hollow spheres with only stem cells—no brain cells, arm cells, heart cells, nerve cells, or any other kind of cell. The term "embryo" activates an image of a little child, which is not what is in frozen form, nor is it used in stem cell research. The picture reinforces the idea that little babies are what are used in stem cell research. Conservative language experts have for years been insisting that it be called "embryonic" stem cell research to reinforce this image; they now insist on using the term "rescue" and have begun to call these embryos "preborn babies." It's like calling an acorn a "preborn oak tree."

The result is that the photo tells a rescue story, which has embedded in it the same "community activist" story frame that we saw above. Here the parents are the activists who brought attention to the problem and began "adopting children"—they did all that they could. Indeed, the evil Congress went so far as to support stem cell research. With persistence and determination, these parents brought it to the attention of the president, who is now stepping in, making government policy. The president's veto is rescuing children, like the ones shown behind him, from stem cell research. There are two kinds of rescuers in this story— the parents and the president.

This photo, with its rescue story, thus makes a political argument: Stem cell research is immoral. It kills children. The government, in its responsibility to protect the security of its citizens, should stop such research. Notice that this type of photo and argument generalize to abortion, too.

You can bet that had a president supportive of stem cell research signed the bill into law, he would have had the photo taken in front of a group of people with Parkinson's disease, MS, Alzheimer's, or a host of other diseases that could potentially be cured through stem cell research. President Bush could not have had such sufferers of disease in the photo. It would have told a very different story and argued for a different position.

ARGUING NET NEUTRALITY

We are constantly faced with new cases and new issues. How do we know what constitutes a progressive versus a conservative argument or narrative? How do we make up new arguments and stories when faced with a new situation? The answer is learning to frame—the progressive deep frames, the moral worldview, the values, the principles, and the general argument frames and narrative frames. We don't mean learning by memorizing but rather learning by acquaintance and by doing. But having it all explicitly laid out helps.

Let's look at the new controversy over "Net neutrality." The arguments—conservative and progressive—were constructed in short order to fit the two systems of values and principles.

We begin with Google's argument in favor of Net neutrality.[5]

> Network neutrality is the principle that Internet users should be in control of what content they view and what applications they use on the Internet. The Internet has operated according to this neutrality principle since its earliest days. Indeed, it is this neutrality that has allowed many companies, including Google, to launch, grow, and innovate. Fundamentally, Net neutrality is about equal access to the Internet. In our view, the broadband carriers should not be permitted to use their market power to discriminate against competing applications or content. Just as telephone companies are not permitted to tell consumers who they can call or what they can say, broadband carriers should not be allowed to use their market power to control activity online. Today, the neutrality of the Internet is at stake as the broadband carriers want Congress's permission to determine what content gets to you first and fastest. Put simply, this would fundamentally alter the openness of the Internet.

Eric Schmidt, Google's CEO, continues the argument, using the "information superhighway" metaphor:

> Today the Internet is an information highway where anybody—no matter how large or small, how traditional or

unconventional—has equal access. But the phone and ca-
ble monopolies, who control almost all Internet access,
want the power to choose who gets access to high-speed
lanes and whose content gets seen first and fastest. They
want to build a two-tiered system and block the on-ramps
for those who can't pay.

The legal, regulatory, and legislative battle is taken up by law
professors Lawrence Lessig and Timothy Wu, representing an ad
hoc group, the Coalition of Broadband Users and Innovators
(CBUI). The CBUI wants the FCC to adopt the following rule:

> A broadband network operator shall not, on a discrimina-
> tory or unreasonable basis, interfere with or impair sub-
> scribers' ability to use their broadband service to access
> lawful Internet content or services, use applications or
> services in connection with their broadband service, or
> attach non-harmful devices to the network.

Thus, the argument for Net neutrality becomes an argument for
government regulation in this form by the FCC.

The issue is new, but we have seen the values, principles,
general argument, and narrative forms before. The Internet is
seen as a commons—part of the infrastructure for the *common
good* developed through the *common wealth* (taxpayer money).
The values are *freedom* (of access) and *equality* (of access). The
government is seen as the protector of freedom and equality
through regulation (via the FCC). Substitute "Internet" for
"parks" or "clean water" or "telephones," and the same argument
applies—government should secure the equal and fair access to
the commons.

The *villains* are the broadband service providers, or BSPs
(e.g., Comcast, Verizon, AT&T, AOL), who own the lines and
control access. Their *crime* is the threat to freedom and equality

for the sake of profit. The *victims* are the citizens using the Internet. The *heroes* are the companies of CBUI (Google, Microsoft, Yahoo), famous spokespeople like Lawrence Lessig, Vint Cerf, and the Internet community itself, especially the bloggers, who have catapulted this issue to national attention.

The conservative side of the argument can be seen in a Cato Institute report and a *Wall Street Journal* editorial. First, Cato begins with cases of what it considers reasonable limitations on Internet content by BSPs:

> It is certainly plausible that BSPs might deny consumers access to Internet content or prohibit attachment of various devices or networks at the edge of the system. Although there are few examples of BSPs engaging in such activities today, there may exist situations in which it is perfectly sensible for a network owner to impose use restrictions or differential pricing schemes on its broadband customers. Network owners may want to discourage the use of certain devices on their networks to avoid system crashes, interference, or "signal theft." They may want to price services differently to avoid network congestion or capture greater revenues on bandwidth-intensive services. They may want to vertically integrate content and conduit on their systems, or partner with other firms that can help them reach new customers and offer superior services. And there might exist scenarios in which blocking access to certain sites makes sense for network operators. They may want to block access to certain controversial websites that contain material some subscribers might find objectionable, or they may want to block sites simply to avoid running the ads of a leading competitor.

Then Cato gets to the *real* rationale behind the industry position—and the rationale that makes the above reasonable:

Net neutrality regulation also flouts the property rights BSPs possess in the infrastructure they own and operate. Worse yet, by ignoring property rights and opening the door to increased regulatory meddling, Net neutrality regulation threatens to retard innovation and investment in new broadband facilities.

Cato is using the conservative argument for the sanctity of property rights—the market is moral and natural, property is the reward for moral action, and property owners have the right to do what they want with their property. Moreover, the market will make everything right. And then Cato gives the "moral market" argument:

Proponents of Net neutrality also tend to ignore the fact that network capacity use and the profit motive will provide very powerful checks on overly restrictive carrier activities. Carriers make money only by carrying more traffic.[6]

And here is *The Wall Street Journal*:

The FCC statement says, "consumers are *entitled*" (our emphasis) to the "content," "applications" and "devices" of their choice on the Internet. They are also "entitled to competition among network providers, application and service providers, and content providers."
    Take a moment to pause over this expansive list of "entitlements." If we take the FCC at its word, access to online pornography is now a right, even though in a different context the FCC is increasingly preoccupied with policing "decency" standards on television. We'd have thought FCC Chairman Kevin Martin would find all that entitlement talk a little embarrassing, given his campaign

for decency standards. . . . Non-discrimination cases could well be brought against Net neutrality backers like Google—say, for placing a competitor too low in their search results. Google's recent complaint that Microsoft's new operating system was anti-competitive is a foretaste of what the battles over a "neutral" Net would look like. Yet Google and other Web site operators have jumped on the Net neutrality bandwagon lest they have to pay a fee to get a guaranteed level of service from a Verizon or other Internet service provider. They don't seem to comprehend the legal and political danger they'll face once they open the neutrality floodgates.[7]

The Wall Street Journal gives the traditional conservative arguments against "entitlements." Nobody is "entitled" to anything given by the government; government handouts are immoral. Moreover, government regulation is dangerous, and companies functioning in the market should know that regulation can be against their self-interest, partly because regulatory agencies may have an opposing agenda (decency standards) and partly because companies can open themselves to lawsuits.

The broadband service providers, in the face of strong opposition from the Internet community, hired Mike McCurry, a public relations specialist, formerly of the Clinton White House. McCurry takes on the blogosphere directly by writing on the Huffington Post:

> The Internet is not a free public good. It is a bunch of wires and switches and connections and pipes and it is creaky. You all worship at Vince [sic] Cerf who has a clear financial interest in the outcome of this debate but you immediately castigate all of us who disagree and impugn our motives. I get paid a reasonable but small sum to argue what I believe. How many of the net neuts out there are honest about the financial resources and special interests

behind your side of the argument? Do you really believe this is good v. evil or just an honest disagreement about what will make the "net flourish and prosper"? What do you make of David Farber's recent caution about the unintended consequences of regulating the Internet?

I am against giving the FCC and other government regulators the power to decide how the Internet will build out in the future. That is what you net neuts are for. The Internet has worked absent regulation and now you want to introduce it for a solution to what? What content is being denied? What service is being degraded? What is not right with the Internet that you are trying to cure?

Instead, you have some myth about dangers ahead if someone actually asks (horrors!) that we pay for the billions it will take to make the Internet to work in the decades ahead? Do you want to pay or do you want to make the giant content companies that will be streaming video and data rich services to pay? I'd rather have a robust Internet that can handle the volume of traffic that we will put on it in the near future rather than a public Internet where we all wait in line for the next pornospammer to let his content go before we get to have arguments like this.

This is not an issue where there is a progressive, pro–little guy, pro-Dem stand versus the big bad companies that pay big bad lobbyists (what a joke you think I am one of them). This is a clear disagreement on principle about what will get us the next generation of the Internet that will work for all of us.[8]

McCurry uses the following strategies:

- Undermine the profit motive arguments against the service providers by accusing the Net neutrality backers (e.g., Vint Cerf of Google) of a profit motive as well. This can't work, because Cerf is a genuine Internet folk hero going back well before Google days.

- Undermine the commons argument by framing the Internet as nothing more than its physical manifestation ("a bunch of wires and switches and connections and pipes and it is creaky"). This can't work, because the savvy Internet community knows that it is a huge amount more—software (especially free open source) and the dedicated work of hundreds of thousands of volunteers.

- Deny that the Internet *is* a commons at all ("The Internet is not a free public good"). Big mistake. Negating the opponents' frame simply reminds them that it has functioned since its inception as a commons, which is what has allowed the huge volunteer effort by its community.

- Deny that this is a battle between greedy big corporations and little guys ("This is not an issue where there is a progressive, pro–little guy, pro-Dem stand versus the big bad companies that pay big bad lobbyists"). Another instance of negating the other guy's frame. He is reminding the Internet audience that this is exactly the issue at hand.

- Reframe the issue as a pragmatic one: Which path will make for an Internet that works better? Invoke the spirit of entrepreneurship and innovation. Ask who should pay—the companies or the people? Here he's representing the right and trying to get support from the left by appearing to move to the left. This can't work, either. This community isn't dumb; they're in the business. If the companies pay, they will pass the charges on to the public plus a lot for their profits. Moreover, the actual plan by the companies is to charge for content right away, on the basis of their previous investments, which are making them a handy profit already.

What we have seen is that (1) the progressive and conservative arguments are just the general argument frames used for a new is-sue, and (2) McCurry tries to reframe in favor of the big corpora-tions and falls into the standard traps.

This should provide some insight about how arguments work. We hope this chapter has been illuminating.

EPILOGUE

There's a reason we called this book *Thinking Points*—because thinking is the activism that comes first. Movements are ultimately about values and ideas. Organizing is crucial, but it has to be *about* something.

This is a handbook for a job that needs to be done—articulating the progressive vision in all of its manifestations over the long term.

Proactively, not reactively.

In grassroots groups all over America. Not just for the next election but indefinitely—election or no election. Win or lose.

A progressive network, an online community, thinking through what you believe and why—and how you can talk to your neighbors.

With the issues of the day discussed not just for their own sake but for how they elaborate the vision, how they contribute to an ongoing dialogue after the issues of the day are forgotten.

Thinking points are the opposite of talking points, the opposite of slogans to parrot, funny bumper stickers, T-shirt mottos, and ad copy. Nothing wrong with them, but that is not what this handbook is about.

Today's issues may be forgotten tomorrow. But the principles and values behind those issues will last.

Yesterday's arguments may never be heard again. But the argument frames that spell out the logic of progressive thought will endure.

The surface frames fade; the deep frames are indelible.

NOTES

1. WINNING AND LOSING

1. Dick Wirthlin and Wynton C. Hall, *The Great Communicator: What Ronald Reagan Taught Me About Politics, Leadership, and Life* (Hoboken, N.J.: John Wiley, 2004).
2. For examples, see "Bush Is Not Incompetent," www.rockridgeinstitute.org/research/lakoff/incompetent.

2. BICONCEPTUALISM

1. Jerome A. Feldman, *From Molecule to Metaphor: A Neural Theory of Language* (Cambridge, Mass.: MIT Press, 2006).
2. Senator Joseph Lieberman's campaign Web site, www.Joe2006.com. Endorsed by the League of Conservation Voters, NARAL, and Planned Parenthood.
3. PBS *NewsHour* interview with Senator Joseph Lieberman, August 11, 2001, www.pbs.org/newshour/bb/politics/july-dec00/lieberman_8-11.html. President George W. Bush has praised Lieberman's stance on Iraq, www.whitehouse.gov/news/releases/2005/12/20051207-1.html.
4. William A. Galston and Elaine C. Kamarck, "The Politics of Polarization" (2005), from the Third Way Middle Class Project, www.third-way.com/products/16.
5. David Sirota, "Find Your True Center," *The Washington Post*, June 11, 2006, www.washingtonpost.com/wp-dyn/content/article/2006/06/09/AR2006060902000.html.

3. FRAMES AND BRAINS

1. Erving Goffman, *Frame Analysis* (New York: Harper, 1974).
2. One example is Framenet, a linguistics research site, framenet.icsi.berkeley.edu/.

3. A comparison of our approach to framing and that of Republican messaging strategist Frank Luntz can be found on our Web site: "Framing vs. Spin, Rockridge as Opposed to Luntz," www.rockridgeinstitute.org/research/lakoff/luntz.

4. Interview with Secretary Colin Powell, September 13, 2001, www.american rhetoric.com/speeches/powell&lehrer.htm.

5. For a more complete discussion, see "The Framing of Immigration," Rockridge Institute Web site, www.rockridgeinstitute.org/research?Subject=Immigration.

6. See "Framing Katrina," www.rockridgeinstitute.org/research/lakoff/framing katrina; and "Bush Is Not Incompetent."

4. THE NATION AS FAMILY

1. George Lakoff, *Moral Politics: What Conservatives Know That Liberals Don't*, 2nd ed. (Chicago: University of Chicago Press, 2002).

2. For more information on Dobson's child-rearing practices, see www.family .org.

3. For the more detailed analysis, see Lakoff, *Moral Politics*.

4. Q&A session with Warren Buffett at Tuck Investment Club lunch, Omaha, Nebraska, 2005, http://mba.tuck.dartmouth.edu/pages/clubs/investment/WarrenBuffett.html.

5. For more details, see George Lakoff, *Whose Freedom?: The Battle over America's Most Important Idea* (New York: Farrar, Straus and Giroux, 2006).

6. For more details, see John W. Dean, *Conservatives Without Conscience* (New York: Viking, 2006).

7. George W. Bush, joint congressional address, September 20, 2001, www.whitehouse.gov/news/releases/2001/09/20010920-8.html; George W. Bush, State of the Union address, January 29, 2002, www.marchforjustice.com/unplugged.php.

8. For a more detailed analysis, see Lakoff, *Whose Freedom?*, Chap. 8; Thomas Frank, *What's the Matter with Kansas?: How Conservatives Won the Heart of America* (New York: Metropolitan Books, 2004).

5. MORALITY AND THE MARKET

1. Adam Smith, *An Inquiry into the Nature and Causes of the Wealth of Nations*, Book II (1776).

2. PBS *NewsHour* interview with Jeffrey Kaye, "Aid for Airlines," February 12, 2002, www.pbs.org/newshour/bb/transportation/jan-june02/airline_aid _2-12.html.

3. Michael Grunwald and Juliet Eilperin, "Energy Bill Raises Fears About Pollution, Fraud Critics Point to Perks for Industry," *The Washington Post*, July 30, 2005, www.washingtonpost.com/wp-dyn/content/article/2005/07/29/AR2005072901128.html.

NOTES   155

4. Michael Pollan, *The Omnivore's Dilemma: A Natural History of Four Meals* (New York: Penguin, 2006).
5. Marketplace Public Radio interview with Robert Reich, "Estate Tax Repeal? Bad for the Economy," June 7, 2006, http://marketplace.publicradio .org/shows/2006/06/07/AM200606071.html.

6. FUNDAMENTAL VALUES

1. George W. Bush on the Marriage Protection Amendment, June 5, 2006, www.whitehouse.gov/news/releases/2006/06/20060605-2.html.
2. Walter Bryce Gallie, paper delivered to the Aristotelian Society, March 12, 1956.
3. Alan Schwartz, "Contested Concepts in Cognitive Social Science" (honors thesis, University of California, Berkeley, 1992). Lakoff, *Moral Politics, Whose Freedom?*
4. The full text of Proposition 209 can be found at www.acri.org/209/209text .html.
5. The full text of Bush's second inaugural address can be found at www .whitehouse.gov/news/releases/2005/01/20050120-1.html.
6. www.falwell.com.
7. www.family.org.
8. The full text can be found at www.hpol.org/lbj/civil-rights/.
9. For an example, see David Brooks, "Of Love and Money," *The New York Times*, May 25, 2006.

7. STRATEGIC INITIATIVES

1. George Lakoff, *Don't Think of an Elephant!: Know Your Values and Frame the Debate* (White River Junction, Vt.: Chelsea Green, 2004), pp. 9–33.
2. Thomas B. Edsall, "Conservatives Join Forces for Bush Plans," *The Washington Post*, February 13, 2005, www.washingtonpost.com/wp-dyn/articles/ A19782-2005Feb12.html.
3. For more information, see www.newamericancentury.org/.
4. "Bush Is Not Incompetent," www.rockridgeinstitute.org. See also Project for the New American Century's Statement of Principles, www.newamerican century.org/statementofprinciples.htm.
5. David Sirota, *Hostile Takeover: How Big Business Bought Our Government and How We Can Take It Back* (New York: Crown, 2006).
6. Alexei Barrionuevo and Keith Bradsher, "Sometimes a Bumper Crop Is Too Much of a Good Thing," *The New York Times*, December 8, 2005.
7. For discussion, see www.sarep.ucdavis.edu/concept.htm.
8. Pollan, *Omnivore's Dilemma*.
9. Ibid.
10. John Locke, "The True Original, Extent, and End of Civil-Government," Second Treatise, *Two Treatises of Government* (1689).

11. Peter Barnes, *Capitalism 3.0: A Guide to Reclaiming the Commons* (San Francisco: Berrett-Koehler, 2006).
12. For more information on transit, see www.publictransportation.org/reports/asp/better_health.asp.

8. THE ART OF ARGUMENTS

1. For the full speech, see http://obama.senate.gov/press/060607-remarks_by_senator_barack_obama_on_the_paris_hilton_tax_break/index.html.
2. Robert Reich, "Story Time," *The New Republic*, March 28, 2005.
3. Beth Schulman, "Restore the Promise of Work: Raise the Minimum Wage," forums.oneamericacommittee.com/index.php?showtopic=30.
4. www.goldmanprize.org/node/100.
5. www.google.com/help/netneutrality.html.
6. www.techlawjournal.com/topstories/2004/20040112.asp; www.cato.org/pubs/pas/pa507.pdf.
7. www.opinionjournal.com/editorial/feature.html?id=110008391.
8. www.huffingtonpost.com/mike-mccurry/hostile-commentary-and-ne_b_20179.html.

ACKNOWLEDGMENTS

This book could not have been written—indeed, the Rockridge Institute would not exist—without the generosity of our donors. To respect their privacy, we withhold their names, but we hope they understand the depth of our appreciation. We would be remiss not to mention the several institutional supporters that have given at unparalleled levels: the Open Society Institute, the Marguerite Casey Foundation, the Nathan Cummings Foundation, the MoveOn Foundation, and the Wallace Global Fund. If this book justifies the confidence all our donors have shown in us and in our mission, then we have achieved a large measure of success.

We recognize the contributions of those who preceded us at Rockridge and upon whose efforts this book builds. We have also benefited mightily from the time and dedication of countless volunteers. Special thanks go to Kathleen Frumkin for her inspiration, ideas, and understanding. And we are indebted to Emily Plec and Kai Stinchcombe for their thoughtful readings and helpful suggestions.

Finally, we acknowledge the tremendous contribution of our editor, Safir Ahmed, who cleared his schedule and worked with us day and night to enable us to meet our tight deadline. His insights enriched the book while his calm demeanor kept us all on an even keel.

ABOUT THE ROCKRIDGE INSTITUTE

The Rockridge Institute is a think tank dedicated to strengthening our democracy by providing intellectual support to the progressive community. Our goal is to empower people to effect positive change by reframing the public debate and facilitating consensus among the array of progressive voices. Because we believe strongly in the progressive moral vision and in the power of engaged citizens, we serve as a hub for people and organizations to find their common progressive voice.

The publication of *Thinking Points* marks an important milestone for us: It provides the basis for an ongoing project of analysis and activism. We will be forming an online, interactive Rockridge Action Network for groups and individuals around the nation who want to use our materials to speak out proactively and on a regular basis. We will also be extending *Thinking Points* on our Web site—speaking out on issues of the day as well as analyzing the framing of more and more social and political issues and making recommendations for how to frame them better.

The Rockridge Institute writes for the public. We do not sell our services to organizations or individuals. We consider ourselves to be part of a compact with those who read our work and benefit from it. And so we look to our readers to support our work and our mission. Rockridge is a 501(c)(3) tax-exempt, nonprofit research and educational institution. Our Web site contains a link for making secure contributions to us: www.rock ridgeinstitute.org. The Institute does not endorse or oppose any candidate for elected office or support any political party.

Bruce Budner
Executive Director